Ancient History Cookbook

By Meredith Curtis

MEREDITH CURTIS

Contents

Time Began in a Garden

Before the Beginning

"In the beginning, God…" (Genesis 1:1 NASB)

"In the beginning was the Word, and the Word was with God, and the Word was God. He was in the beginning with God. All things came into being through Him, and apart from Him nothing came into being that has come into being. In Him was life, and the life was the Light of men. The Light shines in the darkness, and the darkness did not comprehend it" (John 1:1-5 NASB).

Before time, space, and earth existed, there was the Lord God. He has always existed in three persons: Father, Son, and Holy Ghost.

Creation

"In the beginning, God created the heavens and the earth" (Genesis 1:1 NASB)

"God, after He spoke long ago to the fathers in the prophets in many portions and in many ways, in these last days has spoken to us in His Son, whom He appointed heir of all things, through whom also he made the world" (Hebrews 1:1-2 NASB).

God the Father, Son, and Holy Spirit created the earth and heavens in six literal days.

Day One

"In the beginning, God created the heavens and the earth. the earth was formless and void, and darkness was over the surface of the deep, and the Spirit of God was moving over the surface of the waters. Then God said, 'Let there be light', and there was light. God saw that the light was good; and God separated the light from the darkness. God called the light day, and the darkness He called night. And there was evening and there was morning, one day" (Genesis 1:1-5 NASB)

On the first day of Creation, God created light and separated light from darkness. He declared light 'day' and darkness 'night'.

Day Two

"Then God said, 'Let there be an expanse in the midst of the waters, and let it separate the waters from the waters. God made the expanse, and separated the waters which were below the expanse from the waters which were above the expanse; and it was so. God called the expanse heaven. And there was evening and there was morning, a second day" (Genesis 1:6-8 NASB)

On the second day of Creation, God created the sky be separated waters above from waters below.

Day Three

"Then God said, 'Let the waters below the heavens be gathered into one place, and let the dry land appear'; and it was so. God called the dry land earth, and the gathering of the waters He called seas; and God saw that it was good. Then God said, 'Let the earth sprout vegetation, plants yielding seed, and fruit trees on the earth bearing fruit after their kind with seeds in them'; and it was so. The earth brought forth vegetation, plants yielding seed after their kind, and trees bearing fruit with seeds in them, after their kind; and God saw that it was good. There was evening and there was morning, a third day" (Genesis 1:9-14 NASB)

On the third day of Creation, God gathered the waters together to form seas and created the dry land. He also created all kinds of plants with seeds.

Day Four

"Then God said, 'Let there be lights in the expanse of the heavens to separate the day from night, and let them be for signs and for seasons and for days and years; and let them be for lights in the expanse of the heavens to give light on the earth'; and it was so. God made the two great lights, the greater light to govern the day, and the lesser light to govern the night; He made stars also. God placed them in the expanse of the heavens to give light on the earth, and to govern the day and the night, and to separate the light from the darkness; and God saw that it was good. There was evening and there was morning, a fourth day" (Genesis 1:14-19 NASB)

On the fourth day of Creation, God created the sun, moon, and stars. He gave them to us for signs, season, days, and years.

Day Five

"Then God said, 'Let the waters teem with swarms of living creatures, and let the birds fly above the earth in the open expanse of the heavens.' God created the great sea monsters and every living creature that moves, with which the waters swarmed after their kind, and every winged bird after its kind; and God saw that it was good. God blessed them, saying, 'Be fruitful and multiply, and fill the waters in the seas, and let the birds multiply on the earth.' There was evening and there was morning, a fifth day" (Genesis 1:20-23 NASB)

On the fifth day of Creation, God created swimming and flying creatures, including birds, fish, whales, dolphins, crabs, clams, lobsters, barnacles, and krill.

Day Six

"Then God said, 'Let the earth bring forth living creatures after their kind: cattle and creeping things and beasts of the earth after their kind'; and it was so. God made the beasts of the earth after their kind, and the cattle after their kind, and everything that creeps on the ground after its kind; and God saw that it was good. Then God said, 'Let us make man in Our image, according to Our likeness; and let them rule over the fish of the sea and over the birds of the sky and over the cattle and over all the earth, and over every creeping thing that creeps on the earth.' God created man in His own image, in the image of God He created them; and God said to them, 'Be fruitful and multiply, and fill the earth, and subdue it; and rule over the fish of the sea and over the birds of the sky and over every living thing that moves on the earth.' Then God said, 'Behold I have given you every plant yielding seed that is on the surface of the earth, and every tree which has fruit yielding seed; it shall be food for you; and to every beast of the earth and to every bird of the sky and to every things that moves on the earth which has life, I have given every green plant for food'; and it was so. God saw all that He had made, and behold, it was very good. There was evening and there was morning, the sixth day" (Genesis 1:24-31 NASB)

On the sixth day of Creation, God created all kinds of animals including cattle, bears, tigers, elephants, bunnies, cats, dogs, insects, spiders, snakes, pigs, and lambs. He also created man on the sixth day. Wow! That is a ton of things to create. No wonder He rested on the seventh day.

God created man and woman to be special. They would somehow reflect God the Father, Son, and Holy Spirit. I know that sounds a little confusing. Men and women not only were made in God's image, but they would rule over all the earth and everything that lived in it for the Lord. What a special call!

God made the first man, Adam, in a special way.

"Then the LORD God formed man of dust from the ground, and breathed into his nostrils the breath of life; and the man became a living being. The LORD God planted a garden toward the east, in Eden, and there He placed the man whom He had formed....Then the LORD God took the man and put him into the Garden of Eden to cultivate it and keep it. The LORD God commanded the man, saying, 'From any tree of the garden you may eat freely; but from the tree of knowledge of good and evil you shall not eat, for in the day that you eat from it you will surely die" (Genesis 2:7-8, 15-17 NASB)

"Then the LORD God said, 'It is not good for the man to be alone; I will make him a helper suitable for him.' Out of the ground, the LORD God formed every beast of the field and every bird of the sky, and brought them to the man to see what he would call them; and whatever the man called a living creature, that was its name. The man gave names to all the cattle, and to the birds of the sky, and to every beast of the field, but for Adam there was not a helper suitable for him. So the LORD God caused a deep sleep to fall upon the man, and he slept; then He took one of his ribs and closed up the flesh at that place. The LORD God fashioned into a woman the rib which He had taken from the man, and brought her to the man. The man said, 'This is now bone of my bones, and flesh of my flesh. She shall be called Woman because she was taken out of Man. For this reason, a man shall leave his father and his mother, and be joined to his wife; and they shall become one flesh. And the man and his wife were both naked and were not ashamed" (Genesis 2:18-25 NASB)

The first thing Adam got to do was to name the animals. He had a big job to do in fulfilling his purpose to rule over the entire earth. He needed a helper. God created Eve, the first woman, to be a helper for Adam, the first man.

God also started practice of marriage in the Garden of Eden. He laid down a command for all people who would come after Adam and Eve: a man and a woman should leave their homes, come together and be married to begin a new life.

Day Seven: Resting from His Work

"Thus the heavens and the earth were completed, and all their hosts. By the seventh day God completed His work which He had done, and He rested on the seventh day from all the work which He had done. Then God blessed the seventh day and sanctified it, because He rested from all His work which God had created and made" (Genesis 2:1-3 NASB)

On the seventh day of Creation, God rested. He blessed the seventh day of the week, and made it a special day for men, women, and children to rest from their hard work and spend time with Him.

Life in the Garden of Eden

"Now no shrub of the field was yet in the earth, and no plant of the field had yet sprouted, for the LORD God had not sent rain upon the earth, and there was no man to cultivate the ground. But a mist used to rise from the earth and water the whole surface of the ground. Then the LORD God formed man of dust from the ground, and breathed into his nostrils the breath of life; and the man became a living being." (Genesis 1:5-7 NASB)

God created Adam to work the garden, to plant crops for food. The very first man was a farmer and gardener! There was no rain yet. Every morning a mist rose up to water the plants.

"Out of the ground the LORD God caused to grow every tree that is pleasing to the sight and good for food; the tree of life also in the midst of the garden, and the tree of the knowledge of good and evil. Now a river flowed out of Eden to water the garden; and from there it divided and became four rivers. The name of the first is Pishon, it flows around the whole land of Havilah where there is gold. The gold of that land is good; the bdellium and the onyx stone are there.

The name of the second river is Gihon; it flows around the whole land of Cush. The name of the third river is Tigris; it flows east of Assyria. And the fourth river is the Euphrates" (Genesis 2:8-14 NASB)

The Garden of Eden was beautiful. God chose the plants and trees to be good for food and beautiful to look at.

"Then the LORD God took the man and put him into the Garden of Eden to cultivate it and keep it. The LORD God commanded the man, saying, 'From any tree of the garden you may eat freely; but from the tree of knowledge of good and evil you shall not eat, for in the day that you eat from it you will surely die" (Genesis 2:15-17 NASB)

There were two important trees in the Garden of Eden.

The Tree of Life gave them the life and health they needed to live forever.

The Tree of the Knowledge of Good and Evil was forbidden. Adam and Eve were not allowed to eat from it.

The Fall of Man

"Now the serpent was more crafty than any beast of the field which the LORD God had made. And he said to the woman, 'Indeed has God said, "You shall not eat from any tree of the garden"?' The woman said to the serpent, 'From the fruit of the trees of the garden we may eat; but from the fruit of the tree which is in the middle of the garden, God has said, "You shall not eat from it or touch it, or you will die."' The serpent said to the woman, 'You surely will not die! For God knows that in the day you eat from it your eyes will be opened, and you will be like God, knowing good and evil.' When the woman saw that the tree was good for food, and that it was a delight to the eyes, and that the tree was desirable to make one wise, she took from its fruit and ate; and she gave also to her husband with her, and he ate. Then the eyes of both of them were opened, and they knew that they were naked; and they sewed fig leaves together and made themselves loin coverings.

"They heard the sound of the Lord walking in the garden in the cool of the day, and the man and his wife hid themselves from the Presence of the LORD God among the trees of the garden. Then the LORD God called to the man, and said to him, 'Where are you?' He said, 'I heard the sound of You in the garden, and I was afraid because I was naked; so I hid myself.' And He said, 'Who told you that you were naked? Have you eaten from the tree of which I commanded you not to eat?' The man said, 'The woman whom You gave to be with me, she gave me from the tree, and I ate.' Then the LORD God said to the woman, 'What is this you have done?' And the woman said, 'The serpent deceived me, and I ate.'

"The LORD God said to the serpent, 'Because you have done this, cursed are you more than all cattle, and more than every beast of the field; on your belly you will go, and dust you will eat all the days of your life; and I will put enmity between you and the woman, and between your seed and her seed; he shall bruise you on the head, and you shall bruise him on the heel.' To the woman he said, 'I will greatly increase your pain in childbirth, in pain you will bring forth children; yet your desire will be for your husband, and he will rule over you.' Then to Adam He said, 'Because you have listened to the voice of your wife, and have eaten from the tree about which I commanded you, saying, 'You shall not eat from it'; Cursed is the ground because of you; in toil you will eat of it all the days of your life. Both thorns and thistles it shall grow for you; and you will eat the plants of the field; by the sweat of your face you will eat bread, till

you return to the ground because from it you were taken; for you are dust, and to dust you shall return" (Genesis 3: 1-19 NASB).

Eve listened to the lies of the serpent and sinned against the Lord by eating from the Tree of the Knowledge of Good and Evil. Adam listened to Eve's prodding and sinned against the Lord by eating from the Tree of the Knowledge of Good and Evil too.

God punished the serpent, Eve, and Adam. Life would no longer last forever. There would be death. Sin entered the world. How sad.

But even in the midst of such horror, God made a promise.

"And I will put enmity between you and the woman, and between your seed and her seed; he shall bruise you on the head, and you shall bruise him on the heel" (Genesis 3: 15 NASB).

God was making a promise that through the seed of a woman, the Messiah would come to defeat satan.

The LORD God also had to kick Adam and Eve out of the Garden of Eden, but first he made them clothes.

"Now the man called his wife's name Eve, because she was the mother of all the living. The LORD God made garments of skin for Adam and his wife, and clothed them. Then the LORD God said, 'Behold, the man has become like one of Us, knowing good and evil; and now, he might stretch out his hand, and take also from the tree of life, and eat, and live forever'—therefore the LORD God sent him out form the garden of Eden, to cultivate the ground from which he was taken. So He drove the man out; and at the east of the garden of Eden He stationed the cherubim and the flaming sword which turned every direction to guard the way to the tree of life" (Genesis 3: 20-24 NASB).

How sad, Adam and his wife traveled toward an unknown destination. God set an angel to guard the entrance to Eden, so that no person could again eat from the Tree of Life.

But, the Messiah would come and He would make a way for His Chosen People to eat from the Tree of Life again in Heaven.

Life Outside the Garden

"Now the man had relations with his wife Eve, and she conceived and gave birth to Cain, and she said, 'I have gotten a manchild with the help of the LORD.' Again, she gave birth to his brother Abel. And Abel was a keeper of the flocks, but Cain a tiller of the ground. So it came about in the course of time that Cain brought an offering to the LORD of the fruit of the ground. Abel, on his part also brought of the firstlings of his flock and of their fat portions. And the Lord had regard for Abel and his offering; but for Cain and his offering He had no regard. So Cain became very angry and his countenance fell. Then the LORD said to Cain, 'Why are you angry? And why has your countenance fallen? If you do well, will not your countenance be lifted up? And if you do not do well, sin is crouching at the door; and its desire is for you, but you must master it.' Cain told Abel his brother. And it came about when they were in a field, that Cain rose up against Abel his brother and killed him." (Genesis 4:5-7 NASB)

Good news: Adam and Even had two baby boys: Cain and Abel. Cain grew up to be a farmer and Abel grew up to be a shepherd.

We also learn that the practice of making offerings to the Lord was going on. Abel seemed to get it. He offered up a sacrifice of the lives of some of his lambs. Cain brought some of his produce, but that was not what God was looking for. Instead of getting right with God, Cain got angry at Abel.

Bad news: Cain killed his brother and was sentenced to be a wanderer on the earth.

"Then Cain went out from the presence of the LORD, and settled in the land of Nod, east of Eden" (Genesis 4:16 NASB)

Cain left his parents and siblings, with his wife to wander. Cain built the first city,

naming it after his son Enoch. His descendants became musicians, bronze workers, iron workers, and ranchers. This was all before the flood. (Genesis 4:17-22)

Meanwhile, back to Adam and Eve. They had several children, but were given a special son to replace Abel named Seth. When Seth grew up, married, and had his own son, Enosh, men began to call upon the LORD again (Genesis 4:26) We don't know if Abel's murder and Cain's banishment scared people and they stopped worshipping the LORD for a season, but somehow the earlier practice of making offerings to God took a long pause.

From Adam to Noah

The following information is taken from Genesis 5.

At the age of 130, Adam became the father of Seth, as well as other sons and daughters. He died at the age of 930.

At the age of 105, Seth became the father of Enosh, as well as other sons and daughters. He died at the age of 912.

At the age of 90, Enosh became the father of Kenen, as well as other sons and daughters. He died at the age of 905.

At the age of 75, Kenen became the father of Mahalalel, as well as other sons and daughters. He died at the age of 910.

At the age of 65, Mahalalel became the father of Jared, as well as other sons and daughters. He died at the age of 895.

At the age of 162, Jared became the father of Enoch, as well as other sons and daughters. He died at the age of 962.

At the age of 65, Enoch became the father of Methuselah, as well as other sons and daughters. He did not die. *"Then Enoch walked with God; and he was not, for God took him"* (Genesis 5:24 NASB).

At the age of 187, Methuselah became the father of Lamech, as well as other sons and daughters. He died at the age of 969.

At the age of 182, Lamech became the father of Noah, as well as other sons and daughters. He died at the age of 777.

Garden of Eden Layer Salad

6 Cups Chopped Lettuce

Salt and Pepper

6 Egg, hard boiled and sliced

2 Cups Frozen Peas, thawed

1 Pound Bacon, crisp-cooked, drained, and crumbled

2 Cups (8 ounces) Shredded Cheddar Cheese

1 Cup Mayonnaise

2 Tbsp. Sugar

1/4 Cup Sliced Green Onions

Paprika

Place 3 cups of the lettuce in bottom of large bowl; sprinkle with salt and pepper. Layer egg slices over lettuce in bowl and sprinkle with more salt and pepper. Continue to layer vegetables in this order: peas, remaining lettuce, crumbled bacon, and shredded cheese, along with light sprinklings of salt and pepper. Combine mayonnaise and sugar; spread over top, spreading to edge of bowl to cover entire salad. Cover and chill 24 hours or overnight. Garnish with green onion and a little paprika. Toss before serving.

Garden of Eden Berry & Cran-Raisin Salad

Bag of Salad Greens

Green Onions, chopped

Blueberries

Strawberries

Mandarin oranges

Bag Cran-Raisins

Rice Noodles   (Publix has them)

Feta Cheese

Pine Nuts

Mix ingredients together in large salad bowl. Add dressing at the last minute before serving.

Salad Dressing

½ Cup Sugar

½ Cup Apple Vinegar

½ Cup Oil

Mix all ingredients together and pour on salad right before serving.

Eve's Apple & Walnut Salad

Five Apples, peeled, sliced, and soaked in lemon juice

1 Stalk Celery, chopped finely

½ Cup Walnuts, chopped

½ Cup Raisins

½ Cup Golden Raisins

½ Cup Mayonaise

1 tsp Cinnamon

Mix mayonnaise and cinnamon together. Mix fruit and walnuts together and mix with mayonnaise. Toss lightly. Chill.

Seth's Favorite Fruit Salad

3 Bananas, sliced

3 Bunches Grapes, sliced

5 Peaches, sliced

5 Oranges, sectioned

1 Cup Blueberries

1 Cup Strawberries, sliced

1 Melon, cubed

Mix all ingredients together. Serve.

Time Began in a Garden Reading & Listening

The Mystery of History Volume I: Creation to the Resurrection by Linda Lacour Hobar (Bright Ideas Press) Chapters 1-3

Ancient Civilizations & The Bible by Diana Waring (Answers in Genesis) Unit 1

Streams of Civilization Volume I by Mary Stanton & Albert Hyma (Christian Liberty Press) Introductions & Chapter 1

History of the World in Christian Perspective by Jerry H. Combee (A'Beka Book) Chapter 1

Adam and His Kin: The Lost History of Their Lives and Times by Ruth Beechick (Arrow Press)

Finding our Roots in Genesis by Ruth Beechick (Mott Media)

Audio CDs

What in the World is Going on Here? Volume 1: Ancient Civilizations and the Bible Disc 1 Track 1, 2, 3

True Tales Volume 1: Ancient Civilizations and the Bible Disc 1 Track 1-4

Movies

Unlocking the Mystery of Life (Illustra Media)

Icons of Evolution (Illustra Media)

Time Began in a Garden Menu

Lunch (all fruits & veggies)

Garden of Eden Salad

Seth's Favorite Fruit Salad

Eve's Apple & Walnut Salad

Fruit Smoothies

It Began to Rain

God Calls The World to Repentance

"Then the LORD saw that the wickedness of man was great on the earth, and that every intent of the thoughts of his heart was only evil continually. The LORD was sorry that He had made man on the earth, and He was grieved in His heart. The LORD said, 'I will blot out man whom I have created from the face of the land, from man to animals to creeping things to birds of the sky; for I am sorry that I have made them.' But Noah found favor in the eyes of the LORD. These are the records of the generations of Noah. Noah was a righteous man, blameless in his time; Noah walked with God. Noah became the father of three sons: Shem, Ham, and Japheth. Now the earth was corrupt in the sight of God, and the earth was filled with violence. God looked on the earth, and behold, it was corrupt; for all flesh had corrupted their way upon the earth" (Genesis 6:5-12 NASB).

The earth was filled with evil everywhere you turned. Violence and sexual sin are mentioned in Genesis 6 and it seemed that only one man found favor with God. Noah was a preacher of righteousness. God had a job for Him to do that would make it possible for mankind to live on.

"Make for yourself an ark of gopher wood; you shall make the ark with rooms, and shall cover it inside and out with pitch. This is how you shall make it: the length of the ark three hundred cubits, its breadth fifty cubits, and its height thirty cubits. You shall make a window for the ark, and finish it to a cubit form the top; and set the door of the ark in the side of it; you shall make it with lower, second, and third decks. Behold, I, even I am bringing the flood of water upon the earth, to destroy all flesh in which is the breadth of life, from under heaven; everything that is on the earth shall perish. But I will establish my covenant with you; and you shall enter the ark—you and your sons and your wife, and your sons' wives with you. And of every living thing of all flesh, you shall bring two of every kind into the ark, to

keep them alive with you; they shall be male and female. Of the birds after their kind, and of the animals after its kind, two of every kind will come to you to keep them alive. As for you, take for yourself some of the food which is edible, and gather it to yourself; and it shall be for food for you and for them.' Thus Noah did; according to all that God had commanded him, so he did" (Genesis 6:14-22 NASB).

So, Noah and his sons built an ark exactly the way God told Noah to build it. Once he built the ark, he had to gather animals and food for their journey. Imagine how people must have laughed at him. He was building a huge zoo inside a ship. What kind of crazy man would build a boat in the middle of dry land?

"By faith Noah, being warned by God about things not yet seen, in reverence prepared an ark for the salvation of his household, by which he condemned the world, and became an heir of the righteousness which is according to faith" (Hebrews 11:7 NASB).

"If God did not spare angels when they sinned, but cast them into hell and committed them to pits of darkness reserved for judgment; and did not spare the ancient world, but preserved Noah, a preacher of righteousness, with seven others,

when He brought a flood up on the world of the ungodly; ... then the LORD knows how to rescue the godly from temptation..." (2 Peter 2:4, 5, 9 NASB).

Noah preached righteousness as he built the ark with his sons, but no one listened. He warned that it would rain, but you see no one had ever seen rain. They did not know what on earth Noah was saying. Or maybe they just did not want to understand and be accountable for their sins. God gave all of mankind the chance to repent, but in the end, only eight people survived a worldwide flood. Until the day of the first raindrop, people continued on with life as usual.

"For in those days before the flood they were eating and drinking, marrying and giving in marriage, until the day Noah entered the ark" (Matthew 24:38 NASB).

The Flood

When Noah, was 600 years old, everything was ready. He gathered the animals, food, and his family and got on board the ark. For seven days, they waited. Then, came the rain. (Noah 7:6-10)

It rained for forty days and forty nights. (Genesis 7:12) For 150 days, the water covered the earth. (Genesis 7:24)

"God caused a wind to pass over the earth, and the water subsided. Also the fountains of the deep and the floodgates of the sky were closed, and the rain from the sky was retrained; and the water receded steadily from the earth, and at the end of 150 days, the water decreased. In the seventh month, on the seventeenth day of the month, the ark rested on the mountains of Ararat. The water decreased steadily until the tenth month; in the tenth month, on the first day of the month, the tops of the mountains became visible" (Genesis 8:1-5 NASB).

While God was stopping the flood and causing the waters to recede, Noah and his family were eager to get off the boat. First, Noah sent out a raven. Next, Noah sent out a dove, but the dove returned. The second time the dove was sent out, she returned with an olive leaf. The third time Noah sent out the dove, the dove did not return. (Genesis 8)

Finally, God spoke to the family and told them to come out with all the animals. Noah immediately built an altar and sacrificed to the Lord. This pleased the Lord. (Genesis 8) God made a covenant with Noah requiring mankind to be fruitful and multiply, punish murder with the life of the murderer, and enjoy freedom to eat animals for food. (Genesis 9) God also gave a rainbow as a sign of this covenant, that the LORD would never again destroy the entire world with a flood.

As soon as they got settled, Noah planted a vineyard and you can read the rest of that story in Genesis 9. Noah lived to be 950 years old and his descendants would repopulate the world.

We can only imagine that there were many changes in the earth before and after the flood. For one thing, there was no rain before the flood and since the flood, it rains. There are many theories about life before and after the flood, but suffice to say, there were huge changes and one change was that men and women's lifespans became much shorter.

The Ice Age

As rain fell during the Flood of Noah's day, the fountains of the deep were opened and water gushed forth. Was this accompanied by volcanic activity too? At the very least, this water gushing out was much hotter than the water flowing through the seas. Warm water evaporates more quickly than cooler water. This excessive evaporation caused frequent violent storms. As the water condensed, it fell as snow. This cycle escalated until the snow piled up into glaciers and polar caps. The Ice Age had begun! With so much water stored as ice, the water level in the oceans went down exposing continental shelves, which created land bridges. When the Ice Age ended, the water level in the oceans went up again and the land bridges disappeared, dividing the continents again.

Dinosaur Eggs

This recipe for Brazilian Cheese Bread (Pao de Queijo) ends up with little cracks that make the little rolls look like dinosaur eggs.

1 Cup Whole Milk

4 Tablespoons Butter, melted

¼ Cup Vegetable Oil

3 ½ Cups Tapioca Flour + 2 Tbsp.

2 Eggs, slightly beaten

1 Cup Grated Mozzarella Cheese

2-3 Tbsp. Grated Cheddar Cheese

Salt to Taste

Preheat oven to 350°F. Mix milk, salt, vegetable oil, and butter together in a pan and bring to a boil. Immediately remove from heat and mix in tapioca flour. Stir in eggs and cheese. Mix well. Let mixture cool for 15-30 minutes, so that it will be easier to handle. Flour hands and form dough into small balls. Place on baking sheet and bake rolls for 20 to 25 minutes. The rolls will puff up with lots of cracks and yellow flecks and look like a dinosaur egg hatching. Serve warm.

Noah's Grape Ambrosia

Noah planted a vineyard after this Ark Adventure. Here is a recipe with grapes.

2 Cups Grapes

½ Cup Vanilla Yogurt

Mix grapes and vanilla yogurt together and serve chilled.

Pterodactyl Wings

12 Chicken Wings (since Pterodactyls are extinct, use chicken wings….pterodactyl tasted like chicken!)

1Jar BBQ Sauce, flavor of your choice

In a large greased baking pan, lay wings down and coat generously with BBQ sauce on each side. Let wings marinate for 2 hours. Broil wings for 10 minutes each side.

Dinosaur Slaw

6-8 Large Kale Leaves, washed

½ Olive Oil

2 Large Garlic Cloves, finely minced

4 Tbsp. Vinegar

1 ½ tsp. Kosher Salt

1 1/3 Cups Finely Grated Parmesan, plus extra for sprinkling

Strip off Kale leaves and discard stems. Stack leaves and use a sharp knife to make thin slices of Kale.

In a small pan, heat oil over medium heat and sauté garlic until it almost browns. Add salt and vinegar. Stir while vinegar sizzles for a one minute. Pour dressing over kale and toss thoroughly. Mix in Parmesan cheese. Serve with extra Parmesan cheese to sprinkle while people are eating.

Iced Coffee

½ Cup Sugar

1 Cup Water

½ tsp. Vanilla Extract

1 Cup Strong Coffee at Room Temperature

4 Tbsp. Whipping Cream

Make a syrup of water and sugar by heating over medium heat until sugar dissolves. Take off heat and add vanilla. Fill a cup with ice, add syrup, coffee, and whipping cream.

Ice Age Slushies

2 Cups Ice Water

1 Packet Fruit-Flavored Drink Mix (use your favorite flavor)

2/3 Cup Sugar

4 Cups or 1 Full Tray of Ice Cubes

Put all of the ingredients into your blender. Blend on high for a full minute. Stop the blender, use a spoon to stir. Look for unchopped ice chunks. If all the chunks are grated up, then go ahead and serve it. You may need to process it for another full minute though. Serve immediately.

EZ Rainbow Cake

The first rainbow appeared after the Great Flood. It was to always be a reminder that God will not flood the entire earth again with a flood as judgment for mankind's sin.

3 Packages White Cake, prepared according to package directions

Red Food Dye

Orange Food Dye

Yellow Food Dye

Green Food Dye

Blue Food Dye

Purple Food Dye

6 Cake Pans

Divide cake batter into 6 separate bowls and add a different color of food dye to each one. Mix dye in thoroughly. You should have six different colors of cake batter. Pour each colored batter into a separate cake pan and bake according to package directions.

Starting with the purple layer, remove from pan, place on cake pan and frost with white icing. Place the blue layer on next and frost with while icing. Continue with each cake layer: green, yellow, orange, and, finally, red.

Finally, frost the entire cake with white icing.

Rainbow Jell-O® Cups

1 Package Purple Gelatin Mix

1 Package Blue Gelatin Mix

1 Package Green Gelatin Mix

1 Package Yellow Gelatin Mix

1 Package Orange Gelatin Mix

1 Package Red Gelatin Mix

1 Large Container Whipped Topping

Clear Plastic Cups

Dissolve purple gelatin as directed on the box using quick chill method. Pour a small amount of liquid into each cup and refrigerate, reserving 1/3 cup liquid. Refrigerate for 15-30 minutes, until Jell-O® slightly set. Mix 1/3 cup whipped topping with leftover purple liquid. Pour purple whipped topping on top of partially-set gelatin in each cup. Place all cups in refrigerator and allow to set for 15-30 minutes while you work on the next color: blue.

Repeat this process in the following order: blue, green, yellow, orange, red.

This is a long process and while take you several hours. ☺ Take pictures before they eat their rainbow.

It Began to Rain Reading & Listening

The Mystery of History Volume I: Creation to the Resurrection by Linda Lacour Hobar (Bright Ideas Press) Chapters 1-3

Ancient Civilizations & The Bible by Diana Waring (Answers in Genesis) Unit 1

Streams of Civilization Volume I by Mary Stanton & Albert Hyma (Christian Liberty Press) Introductions & Chapter 1

History of the World in Christian Perspective by Jerry H. Combee (A'Beka Book) Chapter 1

In the Days of Noah by Gloria Clannan (Master Books)

Life in the Great Ice Age by Michael and Beverly Oard (Master Books)

Mystery of the Ark: The Dangerous Journey to Mount Ararat by Paul Thomsen (Institute for Creation Research)

The Lost Kingdom by Clint Kelly (Thomas Nelson)

Dinosaurs in God's World and Long Ago By Henrietta D Gambill (Standard Publishing)

What Happened to the Dinosaurs? by John Morris and Ken Ham (Master Books)

Audio CDs

What in the World is Going on Here? Volume 1: Ancient Civilizations and the Bible Disc 1 Track 4-7

True Tales Volume 1: Ancient Civilizations and the Bible Disc 1 Track 5

Digger Deeper Volume 1: Ancient Civilizations and the Bible Disc 1 Track 1-5

Movies

Superbook Noah's Ark (Tyndale House)

It Began to Rain Menu

Lunch

Pterodactyl Wings

Dinosaur Eggs (rolls)

Ice Age Slushies

Rainbow Cake

Lunch

Dinosaur Nuggets (purchase at store)

Noah's Grape Ambrosia

Iced Coffee

Rainbow Jell-O® Cup

Early Civilizations

Tower of Babel & Diversity of Language

For many decades people stayed together, eventually settling on a plain in the land of Shinar. I am sorry to tell you that they build a huge temple to worship demons, or false gods. They worked together to make a name for themselves and build the temple as high into the sky as they could, giving no thought to serving or pleasing God. (Genesis 11)

God, not please, came down and confused their language so that their work could not continue. He also scattered them to the ends of the earth. (Genesis 11)

The Fertile Crescent

Named after the original rivers that bordered the Garden of Eden, the Tigris and Euphrates Rivers were part of a Fertile Crescent (moon-shaped) area of land that was great for growing crops. Its temperate climate made it ideal for culture to flourish. Mesopotamia, or land between rivers, was the land between the Tigris River and the Euphrates River and extending to the other sides of those rivers. Mesopotamia is considered the "Cradle of Civilization." Three ancient empires were birthed in Mesopotamia: Sumer, Assyria, and Babylon.

Sumer

After the Flood, several ancient Sumerian city-nations sprang up in the area including Eridu, Ur, Lagash, Umma, Sippar, Nippur, Uruk, and Kish. Each city was independent, ruling itself. Temples to worship pagan gods, palaces for rulers, and thousands of homes were built inside the sturdy defensive walls. Outside the walls, farms, irrigation canals, and clusters of homes were home to people who lived outside the city. The city was full of hustle-bustle just as cities today are with people selling, buying, and doing all kinds of business with one another.

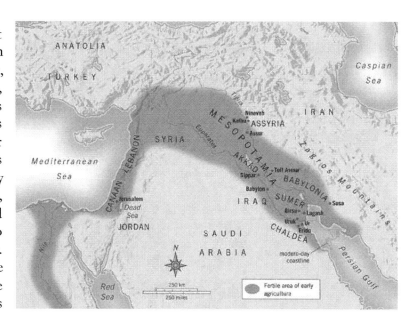

Farmers grew wheat, barley, lentils, rye, cucumbers, lettuce, peas, garlic, carrots, cabbage, beets, radishes, dates, apples, cherries, apricots, plums, grapes, and figs. Oxen helped with the planting while flocks of goats, sheep, and cattle were tended and moved from pasture to pasture. Pigs, cattle, sheep, goats, donkeys, geese, and ducks were domesticated and raised for meat, milk, and to help with the labor.

Ancient Cities in Sumer

When Uruk was excavated, ancient writings from the region (*Epic of Gilgamesh*) were confirmed that one-third of the city was devoted to temple with its pagan worship, one-third of the city was taken up by the palace and government buildings, and the rest of the city was homes and shops.

There were many different jobs in these ancient cities. Bronze workers, silversmiths, goldsmiths, potters, cloth and basket weavers, glassmakers, shoemakers, painters, and sculptors created beautiful and practical items for families. Carpenters, brick layers, and stone masons built buildings and walls. Fishermen, butchers, bakers, and brewers provided food and drink.

Families were the foundation of Sumerian society. Marriage and child rearing were considered a privilege and blessing. Families took care of each other. Girls stayed under the protection and authority of their parents until they were married, helping mothers care for the homes and families. Women could divorce their husbands if they were beaten, cheated on, or neglected.

Children played with jump ropes and balls. Boys enjoyed slingshots and miniature chariots. Girls played with dolls and miniature furniture.

Most homes had several rooms. Tables were a little lower than tables today, but chairs and stools were similar in height. Bed mattresses were filled with goat hair, wool, or palm fiber. Cushions, mattresses, blankets, and sheets were common. Some people slept on reed mats. Belongings were stored in chests or baskets.

Many women wore make-up including lipstick and eyeliner. Tweezers, mirrors, and combs have all been unearthed in archaeological digs. Also discovered from the Sumerian digs were earrings, necklaces, and hair decorations.

Many people usually bathed in the nearest river or canal, but wealthier families had indoor bathrooms with waste being emptied through clay pipes to cesspools near the house. These were the ancient sewers of Sumer.

Scribes in Sumer

Scribes made their living by writing cuneiform, or wedge-shaped, words on clay tablets. Kings dictated to scribes who were quick at writing things down. Letters, lists, inventories, songs for their gods, histories, fables (stories with a strong theme), laments, and epic poems have been unearthed by archaeologists. Often scribes held high positions in royal and wealthy homes where they managed other employees, as well as slaves. Both men and women worked as scribes.

Celebrating Kings with Epic Poems

Many kings were considered to be the "son of a god". In Ancient Egypt, the Pharaoh was considered to be the "son of Ra, the sun god." As a result of this close connection to the dark spirit world, the Sumerian kings were also the high priests of the nation, celebrating religious festivals and offering sacrifices to their pagan idols. In addition, the king commanded the army, often leading the military into battle.

King Sargon the Great created one of the first empires by conquering Uruk, Ur, Lagash, and other cities all the way to the sea (Persian Gulf).

Epic poems celebrated the exploits of powerful kings and warriors. Not only did these tell heroic adventures, but they explored creation, death, loyalty, love, and the spiritual realm. One of the most famous that we have copies of today is the *Tale of Gilgamesh*. The larger than life hero Gilgamesh experiences one exciting adventure after another searching for the secret of immortality. When he finally finds the secret of immortality, it slips through his fingers.

A delightful way to pass historical events on to the next generation is artwork. The Sumerians created mosaics, or pictures made of tiny tiles fit together. The "Royal Standard of Ur" is a mosaic made of shell, limestone, and blue lapis showing a Sumerian army victory and the celebration that followed. Other mosaics commemorated historical events, especially battle victories.

Sumerian Religion

Sumerians did not worship the True God. Instead, they worshipped a wide variety of pagan idols. Enlil was their most powerful god. Utu was the god of the sun, Nanna the moon goddess, Enki god of the water, and Inanna goddess of love.

As I tell you the story, or Sumerian legend, of Enlil, try to figure out what it remind you of. Enlil was walking in the woods one day and saw a lovely goddess named Ninlil. Even though he wasn't married to her, he pretended that she was his wife. The other gods were furious and banished him from the heavenly city to live in the underworld. The child of Enlil and Ninlil was Nanna, the moon goddess. Both Ninlil and Nanna followed Enlil to the underworld, away from the pure heavenly city. What do you think? Does that remind you of the fall of Lucifer from Heaven? Did the Sumerians worship satan?

Divination, or predicting the future, was an important part of their religion. They used animal behavior, animal organs, the location of heavenly bodies, natural disasters, and daily life events. The "behavior" of their pagan gods often resembled the behavior of biblical demons, rather than angels or God Himself. The gods fought with one another. Sometimes the gods hurt humans and sometimes they protected them.

From Noah to Abraham

The following information is taken from Genesis 5 and Genesis 11. Notice how their lifespans get shorter and shorter.

At the age of 500, Noah became the father of Shem, Ham and Japheth. He died at the age of 950.

At the age of 100, Shem became the father of Arpachshad, as well as other sons and daughters. He died at the age of 600.

At the age of 35, Arpachshad became the father of Shelah, as well as other sons and daughters. He died at the age of 438.

At the age of 30, Shelah became the father of Eber, as well as other sons and daughters. He died at the age of 433.

At the age of 34, Eber became the father of Peleg, as well as other sons and daughters. He died at the age of 464.

At the age of 30, Peleg became the father of Reu, as well as other sons and daughters. He died at the age of 239.

At the age of 32, Reu became the father of Serug, as well as other sons and daughters. He died at the age of 239.

At the age of 30, Serug became the father of Nahor, as well as other sons and daughters. He died at the age of 230.

At the age of 29, Nahor became the father of Terah, as well as other sons and daughters. He died at the age of 158.

At the age of 70, Terah became the father of Abraham, Nahor and Haran, as well as, at the very least, another daughter named Sarai, and possibly other sons and daughters. He died at the age of 205.

God Calls Abram Out of a Sumerian City

Abram lived with his father, Terah, in the Sumerian city-state of Ur. Terah had three sons: Abram, Nahor, and Haran. Haran died in Ur, but left a son named Lot. Both Abram and Nahor got married. Abram married his half-sister Sarai. Nahor married his cousin, Milcah, daughter of Haran. (Genesis 11)

Terah took his sons, their wives, and children out of Ur and headed toward Canaan, but they settled down in Haran. Terah died in Haran. (Genesis 11)

Abram had a relationship with God. He loved and served the LORD to the end of his life. God made a promise to Abram that he would bless him and make him a great nation. He was to leave Haran and set out for the land of Canaan. He took his wife, Sarai, his nephew, Lot, and his entire household which included numerous servants and employees. He also took his herds and flocks. He was a very rich man. He and his family lived in tents.

The Patriarchs

Abraham had many adventures with God and had a miracle baby named Isaac. Isaac married his cousin Rebekah and had twin sons, Esau and Jacob. Jacob, chosen by God who changed his name to Israel had thirteen sons: Reuben, Simeon, Levi, Judah, Dan, Naphtali, Gad, Asher, Issachar, Zebulun, Joseph, and Benjamin. The descendants of these sons became the twelve tribes of Israel. Jacob also had a daughter named Dinah.

I encourage you to read about the Patriarchs and their adventures in Genesis chapters eleven through fifty. It is one exciting adventure after another.

Sumerian Food

People ate unleavened bread and porridge made of rye, barley, and wheat. They often mixed sesame seed oil, fish oil, milk, or fruit juice into the dough for variety. There is no record of bees or beekeeping, so honey had to be imported from Egypt and was expensive. Date juice was used to sweeten foods. Fish, deer, gazelle, lamb, beef, pork, geese, and duck were popular, along with fruits and vegetables.

Barley Porridge

Ancient Sumerians wrote on clay tablets. Why not make your own clay tablets.

3 Cups Chicken Broth

2 Onions, chopped

5 Garlic Cloves, minced

1 ½ Cups Barley Flour

Salt to Taste

Bring broth, onions and garlic to a boil. Reduce heat to low and simmer 10 minutes. After 10 minutes, gradually add barley flour little by little so no clumps form. Cook for 15 minutes until porridge is thick. Serve hot.

Barley Flatbread

Ancient Sumerians enjoyed bread and drink made from barley.

2 Cups Barley Flour

2 tsp. Baking Powder

1 tsp. Salt

¾ Cup Water

2 Tbsp. Olive Oil

1 Tbsp. Flaxseed

2 Tbsp. Sunflower Seed

Preheat oven to 400°F and lightly greased a baking sheet. Sift flour, baking powder, and salt into a mixing bowl. Blend water, olive oil, flaxseed, and sunflower seed in a blender until liquefied. Fold liquid into flour mixture. Mix until it forms a dough. Form a circular flat loaf and place on greased baking sheet. Use a knife to score the top of the loaf. Bake for 15-20 minutes. Serve warm with butter.

Prune Bread

Ancient Sumerians love all kinds of fruit: dates, figs, cherries, apricots, apples, plums, and grapes. Prunes are dried plums. Sumerians often mixed fruits into bread. This is an updated recipe.

2 Tbsp. Shortening

½ Cup Sugar

1 Egg

½ Cup Milk

2 Jars Prune Baby Food

1 ½ Cup Flour

1 tsp. Baking Soda

½ tsp. Salt

½ Cup Chopped Almonds

Cream shortening and sugar. Add egg, milk, and prunes. Mix well. Combine flour, baking soda, and salt; add to creamed mixture until just moistened. Stir in almonds. Pour into a greased loaf pans. Bake at 350°F for 30-35 minutes. Cool.

Minoan Fruit Cup

1 Melon

2 Peaches

2 Pears

1 Bunch Red Grapes

½ Cup Almonds, peeled and chopped

1 Bunch Green Grapes

Cut the melon in half and carefully remove the flesh and cut into small pieces. Mix the melon with the rest of the cut fruit, the almonds and the grapes and fill the melon skins with this mixture. Before serving, the fruit should be put in the refrigerator for an hour.

Beef & Carob Stew

Ancient recipes were unearthed in archaeology digs, This recipe used lamb, but since lamb is so expensive, I substituted beef and updated it.

2 lb. Beef Roast

1 Tbsp. Coriander Seeds, freshly ground

3 tsp. Cumin Seed, freshly ground

3 Tbsp. Sesame Oil

6 Medium Shallots, peeled and sliced

2-3 Cups Water

3 Tbsp. Carob Powder

1 tsp. Salt

2 Onion, chopped

6 Cloves Garlic, peeled

1 Cup Yogurt or Sour Cream

Place beef roast in a crock-pot. Sprinkle coriander, cumin, carob powder, and salt on roast. Add onions, garlic, and water. Cook on low 8-10 hours. Mix in yogurt or sour cream before serving.

Esau's Birthright Lentil Stew

Genesis 25:19-34

Lentils might have been one of the very first crops grown in the Fertile Crescent—the area located between the 2 great rivers: the Tigris and the Euphrates. Very popular in the Middle East, the Egyptians and Assyrians found them quite delicious!

2 Cups Lentils

1 tsp. Ground Cumin

4 Tbsp. Oil

1 Cup Beef Broth

1 Large Onion, chopped

1 Large Can Diced Tomatoes

2 Cloves Garlic, minced

Salt and Pepper to taste

Soak lentils in cold water for several hours. Drain. Bring lentils to a boil, reduce heat, and cook for 30 minutes over medium heat. Drain.

Meanwhile, sauté onions and garlic in oil until tender. Add cumin and cook on high for 2 minutes. Stir in broth and lentils. Cook over low heat until lentils are tender. Stir in tomatoes. Add salt and pepper to taste.

Jacob's Ladder Angel Biscuits

Jacob was running for his life, but one night he had a vision of a ladder ascending up into Heaven with angels going up and down.

1 Tbsp. Sugar

1 tsp. Baking Powder

¼ Cup Warm Water

1 tsp. Salt

1 Package Dry Yeast

1 Tbsp. Sugar

2 ½ Cups Flour

½ Cup Shortening

½ tsp. Baking Soda

1 Cup Buttermilk

Preheat oven 400°F. Put sugar and water in small bowl. Add yeast and mix well. Set aside until foamy. Mix together flour, baking soda, baking powder, salt and sugar. Cut shortening into dry ingredients.

Heat buttermilk until lukewarm. Stir yeast mixture into buttermilk. Add this liquid to dry ingredients and mix well.

Turn dough out on floured board. Knead lightly for 3 minutes. Roll the dough out about ¾" thick and cut with a biscuit cutter. Place on a greased pan or cookie sheet. Let the dough rise slightly before baking. Bake 10-15 minutes until lightly browned.

You can mix dough and keep in refrigerator up to 7 days. Mix and store covered. Remove dough from refrigerator 1 hour before you plan to roll it out.

Abraham's Descendants Star Cookies

God told Abraham to look up at the sky and see how many stars were there. God promised to give Abraham as many descendants as stars in the sky.

2 Cups Flour

½ Cup Butter or Margarine, softened

¾ Cup Sugar

1 Large Egg

1/4 tsp. Salt

1 tsp. Vanilla

Star Shaped Cookie Cutters

Preheat oven to 350 degrees. Lightly grease 2 baking sheets. Mix ingredients to form dough. Divide dough into thirds. Work with one third at a time. Roll out dough and cut out with star cookie cutters. Transfer to baking sheets, bake 8 minutes, cool on wire rack and decorate.

Peanut Butter Honey Tablets

Ancient Sumerians wrote on clay tablets. Why not make your own clay tablets.

1 Cup Peanut Butter, smooth

1 Cup Honey

1 Cup Dried Milk

Mix ingredient together. Divide between children and let them form "clay tablets." Using a toothpick, have children write words or draw stick figures.

Early Civilizations Reading & Listening

The Mystery of History Volume I: Creation to the Resurrection by Linda Lacour Hobar (Bright Ideas Press) Chapters 1-3

Ancient Civilizations & The Bible by Diana Waring (Answers in Genesis) Unit 1

Streams of Civilization Volume I by Mary Stanton & Albert Hyma (Christian Liberty Press) Introductions & Chapter 1

History of the World in Christian Perspective by Jerry H. Combee (A'Beka Book) Chapter 1

Priceless Jewel at the Well by Anne Tyra Adams (The Promised Land Diaries/Baker Books)

Magic School Bus: Shows and Tells by Jackie Posner (Scholastic)

Exploring Ancient Cities of the Bible by Michael and Caroline Carroll (Cook Communications)

Crossroads in Time Archaeology Activity Book by Sally Dillon (Andrews University Press)

Audio CDs

What in the World is Going on Here? Volume 1: Ancient Civilizations and the Bible Disc 2 Track 1-2

True Tales Volume 1: Ancient Civilizations and the Bible Disc 2 Track 1-4

Movies

Superbook Jacob & Esau (Tyndale House)

Early Civilizations Menu

Lunch

Barley Porridge

Prune Bread

Minoan Fruit Cup

Lunch

Esau's Lentil Stew

Jacob's Ladder Angel Biscuits

Abraham's Descendant Star Cookies

Lunch

Beef & Carob Stew

Barley Flatbread

Peanut Butter Playdough Tablets

Egypt & Israel

Beginnings of Egypt

Ancient Egypt grew up along the Nile River in northeast Africa. Upper Egypt and Lower Egypt were two different kingdoms that were eventually united by Pharaoh Menes.

From the beginning, the Nile River was important to the Egyptians. Its predictable flooding allowed the people to take advantage of the fertile farmland around the river. They used the river to irrigate land outside of the flood zone, as well as their water highway for transportation. Boats were used to get from place to place and to ship food and building materials.

The Egyptians were amazing builders. Rock quarries yielded massive stones. Surveyors and architects worked hard to choose locations and construct huge projects such as pyramids, temples, and other buildings. Their architecture had its own unique style that other cultures copied. Of course, they became skilled boat builders too with their life centering on the Nile River.

The Egyptians practiced medicine and used mathematics. They blew glass, wrote books, built planked boats, and designed agricultural production techniques to cultivate healthier crops and increase production.

Their dress and artwork was rich with color, jewels, and gold. The ornate combs, bracelets, and necklaces unearthed in archaeological digs reveal the wealth of the Egyptians. Cosmetics were popular, especially eye liner. Statues, figurines, vases, cups, pottery, and religious amulets were beautifully decorated. Gold, lapis, and ivory were used abundantly in Egypt to create opulent jewelry and elaborate works of art.

Egyptian Writing

Hieroglyphs, the Egyptian system of writing, were made accessible to modern scholars with the discovery of the Rosetta Stone in 1799. The rock had the same message from King Ptolemy V in Ancient Egyptian hieroglyphs, Demotic script, and Ancient Greek. This allowed us to translate hieroglyphs and discover remarkable information about Ancient Egypt.

Hieroglyphics contain picture symbols that stood for whole words or sounds, depending on the symbol. The Egyptians used decorative writing for religious purposes.

Pharaohs, Mummies, & Pyramids

Most people divide the history of Ancient Egypt into three periods: Old Kingdom, Middle Kingdom, and the New Kingdom. These kingdoms were strong and prosperous, but between each one was a period of near-collapse called the Intermediate periods.

The Giza Pyramids and the Great Sphinx of Giza were constructed during the Old Kingdom years. The Giza Pyramid was over 400 feet tall and was one of the Seven Wonders of the Ancient World.

There were over 100 pyramids. The earlier pyramids had steps, or ledges, up the sides, but later pyramids have sloping, flat sides. The base of the pyramid is always a perfect square and the building material was most often limestone.

Inside the pyramids is a pharaoh's burial chamber filled with all kinds of treasures. The walls were often painted with beautiful pictures. I am sorry to tell you that the Egyptians believed they could use these things in the afterlife.

While Joshua was leading the people of Israel in the Promised Land, King Tut was reigning in Egypt. King Tut became Pharaoh at the age of seven years old. His father had changed the religious system of the country to worship only one God. Was that the true God? King Tut, under the influence of his advisors, changed the religious system back to the worship of idols. King Tut was an older teenager when he died and seems to have died from a wound to his leg. From studying his mummy, they found a broken leg with a bad infection.

Let's fast forward thousands of years. Howard Carter, an English artist who was homeschooled, went to Egypt in 1891 when he was only seventeen years old. Howard was seeking adventure so he applied for a job as an assistant to an archaeologist going to Egypt. Carter's job was to copy drawings and inscriptions from artifacts to study later. He loved learning about Egypt and soon became an expert. Eventually, he bought and sold antiques too, while continuing to work as an excavator and illustrator. He decided to hunt for the famous King Tut's tomb. With money from a rich man who believed in his project, he hired fifty men to help him. Howard eventually found a long stairway leading down to a secret door. Howard wanted to open the secret access, but instead he sent for his benefactor, Lord Carnarvon to travel to Egypt enter and examine the hidden space together.

Lord Carnarvon and Howard Carter were amazed when they opened the door. The room was filled with glittery treasures: jeweled chests, vases, chariots, and furniture made of gold. The coffin itself was made of gold. King Tut's face was covered with a gold mask. Inside the tomb, there were statues, gold jewelry, chariots, boats, chairs, and paintings. And, of course, the mummy of King Tut.

Mummies were the Egyptian's method of trying to preserve bodies as long as possible. This elaborate process of embalming included removing water and some organs out of the body. The heart was left inside the body and the brain, thought to be useless, was thrown out. The body was covered with a salty substance called natron for forty days to help the body dry out. After it was dry, lotions were used to preserve the outer shell. The body was packed and then wrapped with strips of cloth. After the mummification process was completed, the body was covered with a sheet and put in a sarcophagus, or stone coffin.

In spite of all their advanced technology, the Egypt was subjugated by the Assyrian Empire for a season and 100 years later, was occupied by the Persian Empire. In 332, Alexander the Great conquered Egypt. Egypt also became part of the Roman Empire. So, her glory days ended, but her mysterious lure to people around the world continued throughout history. People in all times and from all places, love to go to Egypt to see the legendary pyramids and other famous sites.

Egyptian Culture

Here are some fun facts about Egyptian culture.

- Egyptians lived in sun baked mud homes. The inside walls were painted with beautiful colors or charming scenery. They slept on the roof in the summer and bathed in the Nile River.
- Both men and women wore make-up as a religious practice, believing it had healing powers. Egyptian inventors were constantly improving make-up.
- Egyptians used calendars, musical instruments, plows for farming, and medicine. They even used toothpaste. They used moldy bread for infections.
- Egyptians wrote with hieroglyphics on papyrus, a kind of paper. They used ink.

I am sorry to tell you that Egyptians did not worship the true God. They worshipped idols. Cats were considered sacred in Ancient Egypt.

Incubation of the Nation of Israel

Joseph, the favorite son of Jacob was intensely disliked by his brothers. They were jealous of his father's affection. One day, they sold him into slavery and Joseph ended up in Egypt. God's favor was upon him and he ended up interpreting a dream for Pharaoh which landed him a prestigious job as second-in-command to Pharaoh himself.

Meanwhile, famine came to Canaan where his father and brothers were living. Their search for food led them to Egypt where they were reunited with their long-lost brother/son Joseph. Joseph urged them to stay in Egypt and they did.

In time, other pharaohs forgot about Joseph and came to despise these shepherds living in the best part of Egypt. They enslaved the Israelites who worked to build pyramids and other national projects. Life became harder and harder. Soon the Israelites cried out to God to rescue them.

By this time the nation of Israel had grown from one large family to 600,000 men plus women and children. The people were healthy and hearty, though they were becoming weary and eager to be free from slavery.

Exodus

God heard the prayers of his people and raised up a deliverer for them. His name was Moses, a humble man who loved the Lord with all his heart.

He went to Pharaoh and asked if his people could be given freedom to go worship God in the desert. Pharaoh refused. From that point on, there was a showdown: Pharaoh and his magicians versus God and His people. After a serious of plagues, the final one was the death of all the firstborn sons in Egypt. The only way to keep death from hitting your household was to kill a lamb, eat it, and wipe the blood on the doorpost of the house. The angel of death passed through Egypt, but did not touch any of the Israelite's homes because of the blood of the lambs. Since the angel of death passed over, the feast celebrated in remembrance of this is called Passover. Passover is still celebrated by Jews today throughout the world.

After this last plague, the Pharaoh relented and allowed the people to flee. A huge group of Israelites hit the road with all their possession bound for the Promised Land with God leading the way. Originally promised to Abraham, this land was flowing with milk and honey. Pharaoh changed his mind and set off after Moses and the Jews. Arriving at a desperate place, the Israelites found themselves between Pharaoh's army and the Red Sea. Miraculously, God parted the Red Sea so that the Israelites could pass over and once they reached the other side, the waters rolled back and drowned Pharaoh's army.

The nation of Israel began a journey to their Promised Land, receiving the Ten Commandments and building a Tabernacle for worship on the way. Unfortunately, their sin postponed their initial arrival time and they had to wander in the desert for 40 years.

Read Exodus, Numbers, Leviticus, and Deuteronomy to learn more about their exciting adventures.

Moses Writes it All Down

God's Holy Book, *The Bible*, continued to be written, passed down carefully to the next generation, until it passed into the hands of Moses. The Holy Spirit inspired Moses who wrote down the words God wanted written down about Israel's adventures in Egypt, their miraculous escape, and the journey to the Promised Land.

Joshua is the Hero and the Writer

Joshua took the helm after Moses died, leading the people to cross the Jordan River into the Promised Land. With a few defeats because of their sin and many victories, they conquered the heathen people to take the land. The Israelites settled down to enjoy their new freedom. Joshua wrote everything down. Read Joshua to learn more about these exciting adventures.

Israel's Saga Continues

After Joshua died, judges ruled the nation of Israel. I am sorry to tell you that the people did what was right in their own eyes instead of obeying the Lord. God would give them over to oppressors to punish their sin until they cried out to the LORD for a deliverer. God would use a hero to rescue them, but soon the Israelites were back in their sin. You can read Judges for the whole story.

The final judge was Samuel, a righteous man without righteous sons to follow in his footsteps. The people began to cry out for a human king even though the Lord was their king. God, saddened by their rejection of him, gave them their first king, Saul. Saul was eventually rejected by God who raised up a king after his own heart, David. David was a mighty warrior who extended the kingdom's boundaries and ruled in righteousness. During his son Solomon's reign, Israel was at the height of her glory with a huge territory, wealth beyond measure, and a wise king who wrote the book of Proverbs. After Solomon's death, the kingdom was split between two kings. One ruled ten tribes from Samaria and was known as Israel. The other king ruled over Judah and Benjamin from Jerusalem and was called Judah. You can read I Samuel, II Samuel, I Kings, II Kings, I Chronicles, and II Chronicles for the full story.

The Old Testament

Book after book in the Old Testament tells the story of the nation of Israel. Their history, poems, songs, and prophetic words were carefully recorded, inspired by the Lord, and preserved for us to read today.

Egyptian Food

Egyptians cooked in clay ovens. They ate bread, barley, wheat, olive oil, butter, milk, cheese, grapes, melons, dates, figs, onions, leeks, celery, lettuce, garlic, beans, peas, lentils, nuts, cucumbers, lamb, beef, fish, duck, quail, pigeon, goose, and goat. Their main drink was made form barley. The Egyptians raised bees for honey. Honey was used to sweeten foods, especially desserts. Mustard, salt, cumin, coriander, honey, dill, and vinegar were used to flavor foods.

Food from the Promised Land

Israelites ate bread, drank wine, and enjoyed a variety of foods including wheat, barley, lentils, olives, chickpeas, peas, squash, leeks, garlic, onions, radishes, endive, watermelon, grapes, figs, dates, pomegranate, carob, quince, almonds, walnuts, pistachios, goat, sheep, quail, partridge, chicken, fish, eggs, goat milk, goat cheese, and honey. Foods were seasoned with cumin, dill, chicory, thyme, ginger, hyssop, coriander, mint, mustard, saffron, capers, and cinnamon.

Promised Land Granola

2 Cups Old-Fashioned Oats

3/4 Cup Slivered Almonds

1/2 Cup Sweetened Flaked Coconut

1/2 Cup Cashews

1/3 c Firmly Packed Brown Sugar

1 1/2 tsp Ground Allspice

1 tsp Ground Cinnamon

1/4 Cup Butter

3 T Honey

1 C Chopped Dates

Preheat oven to 300 F. Mix first 7 ingredients in large bowl. Melt butter with honey in pan over low heat. Pour over granola mixture and toss well. Spread out mixture on cookie sheet.

Bake 20 minutes, stirring occasionally. Add dates; mix to separate any clumps. Continue to bake until granola is golden brown, stirring frequently, about 15 minutes longer. Cool.

Store granola in an airtight container at room temperature.

Cucumber Yogurt Salad

2 Cucumbers, peeled, quartered, and chopped

1 Cup Plain Yogurt

1 tsp. Dill

Salt and Pepper to Taste

Gently mix together the ingredients. Toss lightly and serve!

Spiced Oranges & Raisins

4 Oranges, peeled and sliced

1 Cup Golden Raisins

1 tsp. Cinnamon, ground

1 tsp. Ginger, ground

½ tsp. All Spice, ground

Gently mix together all the ingredients. Toss lightly and serve!

Spiced Dates & Raisins

2 Cups Dates

½ Cup Raisins

1 tsp. Cinnamon, ground

1 tsp. Cloves, ground

Gently mix together all the ingredients. Toss lightly and serve!

Ruth's Barley Squares

Onion, finely chopped

1 Green Pepper, chopped

2 Tbsp. Butter

3 Cups Cooked Barley

2 Eggs, beaten

2 Cups Swiss Cheese, shredded

¼ tsp. Thyme Leaves, crushed

½ tsp. Pepper

Saute onion and pepper in butter. Add the rest of the ingredients and mix well. Spread into a greased casserole dish and bake at 350°F. Prepare pastry. Sprinkle chicken, cheese and onion in pastry-lined pie plate. Beat eggs; beat in remaining ingredients, and pour into pie plate. Bake uncovered 15 minutes. Reduce oven temperature to 300°. Bake until knife inserted in center comes out clean, about 30 minutes longer. Let stand 10 minutes before cutting.

Leek and Onion Soup

5 Tbsp. Olive Oil

3 Large Leeks (white and pale green parts only), sliced

1 ½ Pounds Russet Potatoes, peeled, diced

1 Large White Onion, chopped

4 (14 ½ ounce) Cans Vegetable Broth

3 Large Garlic Cloves, chopped

1 ½ Cups Grated Swiss Cheese

8 Slices Sourdough Bread

½ Cup Chopped Fresh Chives or Green Onion Tops

Heat 4 tablespoons of oil in heavy large pot over medium-low heat. Add leeks, potatoes and onion. Sauté until onion is tender, stirring occasionally, about 12 minutes. Add broth and bring soup to boil. Reduce heat to medium-low. Simmer until all vegetables are tender, about 20 minutes. Working in batches, puree 5 cups soup in blender. Return puree to soup in pot. Season with salt and pepper. This soup can be made 1 day ahead. Refrigerate uncovered until cold. Cover and keep refrigerated.

Preheat oven to 350°F. Stir remaining 1 tablespoon oil and garlic in small skillet over low heat until garlic is fragrant, about 1 minute; remove from heat and cool. Add cheese to garlic in skillet; toss to combine. Arrange bread slices on baking sheet. Spoon cheese mixture onto bread slices, dividing equally. Bake toasts until cheese melts, about 10 minutes.

Bring soup to simmer over medium heat, stirring frequently. Ladle into bowls. Sprinkle generously with chives. Serve, passing toasts separately.

Beef Barley Soup

2 Pound Beef Stew, chopped

2 Medium Onion, chopped

4 Stalks Celery, chopped

4 Carrots, diced

1 ½ Cup Barley

1 Bay Leaf

Salt and Pepper to Taste

12   Cups   Beef   Stock

Combine all ingredients in a crockpot. Cover; cook on low for 6 to 8 hours.

Elijah's Hummus

2 Cups Canned Chickpeas, drained and rinsed

1 Lemon, juiced

2 Tbsp. Tahini Paste

1 Tbsp. Garlic

¼ Cup Olive Oil, plus more, for drizzling

Salt

Freshly Ground Black Pepper

1 Cup Kalamata Olives, pitted

Fresh Pita Bread or Crackers

In a food processor fitted with a metal blade, combine the chickpeas, lemon juice, tahini paste, and garlic. Process mixture until smooth and with the machine running, add 1/4 cup olive oil, a little at a time. Season with salt and pepper. Spoon the hummus in the center of a large platter. Drizzle the hummus with olive oil. Arrange the black olives and fresh pita bread around the hummus. (Yield: 2 cups)

David's Shepherd's Pie

Ground Lamb, Turkey, or Beef, cooked and drained of fat

1 Bag Frozen Peas, Beans, or Corn (pound bag)

Mashed Potatoes

Place ground meat in a greased casserole, top with frozen vegetables. Top with mashed potatoes. Bake at 350 for ½ hour until well heated. Serve with mint jelly

Pharaoh's Okra Stew

8 Large Cubes of Lamb or Beef

1 Onion, peeled and diced

1 tsp. Salt

2 Tbsp. Oil

6 Cloves Garlic, peeled and chopped

3 Tomatoes, diced

3 Cups Frozen Okra

In a pan, add meat, onion, garlic, and enough water to bring meat and onion to a boil. Boil, add salt, and reduce heat. Cover and simmer for 20 minutes. Cut meat cubes smaller. In another pan, heat oil and add garlic, cooking until almost browned. Add tomatoes and juice to garlic. Let simmer for 5 minutes. Add okra and mix well. Add meat and broth, stir in, and bring to a boil. Lower heat and simmer for 30 minutes.

Mummy Dogs

The Egyptians preserved dead bodies with an intricate process that has allowed us to glimpse into the past. This process is called mummification. In the final step the body is wrapped in strips of linen. You can mummify a hot dog with strips of dough and enjoy your own edible mummy.

2 (8oz.) Cans Refrigerated Crescent Rolls, unbaked

8 Hot Dogs

Separate Crescent roll dough into 8 separate rectangles, pressing perforations to seal. Slice each rectangle into 8 long slices. Use slices to wrap, or mummify, each hotdog so that it looks like an Egyptian mummy. Be sure to leave the "face" uncovered. Bake at 375°F for 15 minutes, or until light golden brown.

Egyptian Honey Cakes

4 Cups Cream of Wheat

1 ¼ Cups Butter

1 Cup Sugar

½ tsp. Baking Soda

½ tsp. Baking Powder

1 ¼ Cups Plain Yogurt

½ Cup Blanced Almonds

¼ Cup Honey

Preheat oven to 400°F. Melt butter over low heat and stir in Cream of Wheat and sugar. Blend baking soda and baking powder; stir into yogurt. Add to butter mixture and mix well. Grease baking pan and pour in batter. Using a knife, score the top with diamond shapes and put a blanched almond inside each diamond. Bake for 30 minutes until brown on top.

Scripture Cake

4 ½ Cups Cake Flour (I Kings 4:22)

1 Cup Butter (Judges 5:25)

2 Cups Sugar (Jeremiah 6:20)

2 Cups Raisins (I Samuel 3:12)

2 Cups Figs (Nahum 3:12)

2 Cups Almonds (Numbers 17:8)

½ Cup Sour Milk (Judges 4:19)

3 Tbsp. Honey (I Samuel 14:25)

Pinch of Salt (Leviticus 2:13)

6 Eggs (Jeremiah 17:2)

2 tsp. Baking Soda (Amos 4:5)

Season with spices (II Chronicles 9:9)

Follow Solomon's prescription for making a good boy (Proverbs 3:12) and you will have a good cake. Bake @ 350°F for 1 hour.

Solomon's Honey Sesame Candy

2 Cups Sesame Seeds

1 ¼ Cups Honey

In a heavy pan, cook the honey and sesame seeds together gently for about 8 to 10 minutes, stirring occasionally until the mixture is golden brown. Test in cold water - when a soft ball is formed, the sweet is ready. Pour onto a marble slab or greased pan. Use a rolling pin to flatten mass to about 12-inch thickness. As the candy cools, break into pieces. Wrap the pieces individually in waxed paper and store in a tin box.

Aaron's Rod Almond Candy

Numbers 17:8

Aaron is recognized by God as the chosen leader by having a stick of almond wood bud, blossom, and bear fruit

1 ½ lbs. Vanilla Flavored Candy Coating

1 (14-oz) Can Sweetened Condensed Milk

1/8 tsp. Salt

1 tsp. Almond Extract

1 lb. Toasted Almonds

In a heavy saucepan, over low heat, melt candy coating, condensed milk, and salt. Remove from heat; stir in extract, then almonds. Spread evenly into wax paper-lined pan. Chill until firm. Turn onto cutting board; peel off paper and cut into squares. Store tightly covered at room temperature.

MICROWAVE: In 2-quart glass measure, combine candy coating, condensed milk and salt. Cook on 100% power (high) 3 to 5 minutes, stirring until smooth. Proceed as above.

Abigail's Raisin Cakes

4 Eggs

½ Cup Honey

2/3 Cup Flour

½ tsp. Salt

2 ½ Cups Raisins

1 Cup Almonds

Whipped Cream

Preheat oven to 350°F. In large bowl, beat eggs until fluffy. Add honey, beat well. Add flour, salt, raisins, and almonds, mix well. Pour into a greased pan and bake for 40 minutes. Serve warm with whipped cream.

Yogurt Pound Cake

1 Cup Brown Sugar, Packed

1 Cup Butter (2 sticks), softened

6 Eggs

3 Cups Flour

¼ tsp. Baking Soda

¼ tsp. Salt

1 Cup (8 oz.) Plain Yogurt

½ Cup Poppy Seeds

Apricot Yogurt Frosting

Preheat oven to 325 F. Grease and flour a 10" tube pan. In large bowl, beat sugar and butter until fluffy. Add eggs one at a time. Combine flour, soda, and salt. Add to sugar mixture; alternating with yogurt. Stir in vanilla and seeds. Pour into pan. Bake 90 minutes until toothpick inserted in center comes out clean. Cool 10 minutes on rack. Turn out onto plate and cool completely. Frost with Apricot Yogurt Frosting.

Apricot Yogurt Frosting

4 Cups Powered Sugar

¼ Cup Apricot Preserves

¼ Cup Plain Yogurt

¼ Cup Butter, softened

Pinch Salt

In large bowl, beat all ingredients together until smooth and creamy.

Egyptian Honey Cakes

4 Cups Cream of Wheat

1 ¼ Cups Butter

1 Cup Sugar

½ tsp. Baking Soda

½ tsp. Baking Powder

1 ¼ Cups Plain Yogurt

½ Cup Blanced Almonds

¼ Cup Honey

Preheat oven to 400°F. Melt butter over low heat and stir in Cream of Wheat and sugar. Blend baking soda and baking powder; stir into yogurt. Add to butter mixture and mix well. Grease baking pan and pour in batter. Using a knife, score the top with diamond shapes and put a blanched almond inside each diamond. Bake for 30 minutes until brown on top.

Egypt & Israel Reading & Listening

The Mystery of History Volume I: Creation to the Resurrection by Linda Lacour Hobar (Bright Ideas Press) Chapters 1-3

Ancient Civilizations & The Bible by Diana Waring (Answers in Genesis) Unit 1

Streams of Civilization Volume I by Mary Stanton & Albert Hyma (Christian Liberty Press) Introductions & Chapter 1

History of the World in Christian Perspective by Jerry H. Combee (A'Beka Book) Chapter 1

Tutankhamen by Robert Green (Children's Press)

Tirzah by Lucille Travis (Herald Press)

Mummies, Tombs and Treasure: Secrets of Ancient Egypt by Lila Perl (Sandpiper)

Miriam's Cup: A Passover Story by Fran Manushkin (Scholastic Press)

Learning about the Passover by Barbara Soloff Levy (Dover Publications)

Shadow Hawk by Andre Norton (Bethlehem Books)

Adventures in Ancient Egypt by Linda Bailey (Kids Can Press)

The Golden Goblet by Eloise Jarvis McGraw (Puffin)

The Pharaohs of Ancient Egypt by Elizabeth Payne (Landmark Books)

The Riddle of the Rosetta Stone: Key to Ancient Egypt by James C Giblin (Harper Collins)

Mara: Daughter of the Nile by Eloise Jarvis Mc Graw (Puffin)

Mummies: Made in Egypt by Aliki (Harper Collins)

Kids Discover: Ancient Egypt (Kids Discover Magazine)

The Peaceful Warrior: The Diary of Deborah's Armor Bearer by Anne Tyra Adams (Promised Land Diaries Baker Books)

Hittite Warrior by Joanne Williamson (Bethlehem Books)

Trojan Horse by David Clement-Davies (DK Publishing)

Journey for Tobiyah by Barbara Morgan (Random House)

King Solomon's Navy by Nora Benjamin Kubie (Harper)

Magnifications: The Temple at Jerusalem: From Solomon to Herod and Beyond by Jacqueline Morley and John James (Brighton Book House)

Audio CDs

What in the World is Going on Here? Volume 1: Ancient Civilizations and the Bible Disc 2 Track 5

True Tales Volume 1: Ancient Civilizations and the Bible Disc 2 Track 5, Disc 3 Track 1-2

Digger Deeper Volume 1: Ancient Civilizations and the Bible Disc 2 Track 1-2

Movies

The Ten Commandments (Directed by Cecile DeMille, Starring Charlton Heston)

The Prince of Egypt (Dream Works)

Samson and Delilah (1949—starring Hedy Lamarr)

Egypt & Israel Menu

Lunch

Grapes

Hot Milk with Honey

Promised Land Granola

Yogurt

Yogurt Cake with Frosting

Aaron's Rod Candy

Lunch

Ruth's Barley Squares

Nile Fish Sandwiches

Leek & Onion Soup

Lunch

David's Shepherd's Pie

Abigail's Raisin Cakes

Solomon's Sesame Candy

Lunch

Elijah's Hummus

Pita Bread

Crackers

Cucumber Salad or Sliced Cucumbers

Scripture Cake

Israel, Assyrians, & Babylonians

Assyria

Time moved on and other kingdoms arose. Assyria and Babylon vied for supremacy in the Fertile Crescent. Here is a map of various kingdoms in the Fertile Crescent, as well as Egypt.

The city-state of Assur and Nineveh existed back in Sumerian times and ended up in Sargon the Great's kingdom, the Akkadian Empire. Assyria gets its name from the city-state of Assur. Under the leadership of Sargon the Great and his successors, the area that become Assyria thrived and prospered, enjoyed rigorous trade with other parts of the kingdom, as well as other empires and city-states. After the Akkadian Empire fell, Assyrians enjoyed self-rule once again.

Sometimes Assyria quietly ruled itself. For centuries, however, a power struggle existed between Assyria and Babylon and sometimes Assyria found itself ruling Babylon while other times under its dominion.

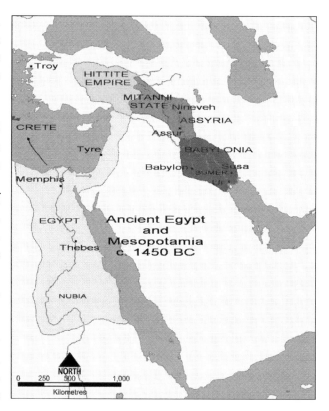

The king of Assyria was the leader of the army as well as the high priest of Ashur, their top idol-god. Known for their well-bred and trained horses, the Assyrians fertile land left them with lots of time to invest in horse ranching. Books on horse breeding and training have been unearthed in archaeological digs. The Assyrians exported horses, lumber, and metal ore.

Assyria became a military powerhouse with all men obligated to serve in the military. One ruler of Assyria, King Arvad, managed to conquer the Phoenician city-states of Tyre, Sidon, Simyra, Beirut, and more. The Assyrians were ruthless killers in battle. Many times, people would commit suicide rather than fall into Assyrian hands as prisoners of war. This ruthlessness spread into their society where laws were harsh, women had few rights, and people were raised to see might as right.

Israel & Assyria

We meet an Assyrian king in II Kings 15.

"In the thirty-ninth year of Azariah king of Judah, Menahem son of Gadi became king over Israel and reigned ten years in Samaria. He did evil in the sight of the LORD; he did not depart all his days from the sins of Jeroboam the son of Nebat, which he made Israel sin. Pul, king of Assyria, came against the land, and Menahem gave Pul a thousand talents of silver so that his hand might be with him to strengthen the kingdom under his rule. Then Menahem exacted the money from Israel, even from all the might men of wealth, from each man fifty shekels of silver to pay the king of Assyria. So the king of Assyria returned and did not remain in the land" (II Kings 15: 17-20 NASB).

And later in the chapter, we meet another Assyrian king.

"In the days of Pekah king of Israel, Tiglath-pileser king of Assyria came and captured Ijon and Abel-beth-maacah and Janoah and Kedesh and Hazor and Gilead and Galilee, all the land of Naphtali; and he carried them captive to Israel" (II Kings 15: 29 NASB).

In Israel none of the kings served the LORD. Eventually, God used the Assyrians to judge the nation of Israel. Assyrians captured the nation and removed the Jews from their land and transplanted people from other nations to live in Samaria, the capital of Israel.

"In the ninth year of Hoshea, the king of Assyria captured Samaria and carried Israel away into exile to Assyria, and settled them in Halah and Habor, on the river of Gozan, and in the cities of the Medes. Now this came about because the sons of Israel sinned against the LORD their God, who had brought them up from the land of Egypt from under the hand of Pharaoh, king of Egypt, and they had feared other gods and walked in the customs of the nations whom the LORD had driven out before the sons of Israel, and in the customs of the kings of Israel which they had introduced. The sons of Israel did things secretly which were not right against the LORD their God. Moreover, they built for themselves high places in all their towns from watchtower to fortified city. They set for themselves sacred pillars and Asherim on every high hill and under every green tree, and there they burned incense on all the high places

as the nations did which the LORD had carried away to exile before them; and they did evil things provoking the LORD. They served idols" (II Kings 17: 6-12 NASB).

"The sons of Israel walked in all the sins of Jeroboam which he did; they did not depart from the them until the LORD removed Israel from His sight, as He spoke though all His servants and prophets. So Israel was carried away into exile from their own land to Assyria until this day. The king of Assyria brought men from Babylon and from Cuthah and from Avva and from Hamath and Sepharvaim, and settled them in the cities of Samaria in place of the sons of Israel. So they possessed Samaria and lived in its cities. At the beginning of their living there, they did not fear the LORD; therefore the LORD sent lions among them which killed some of them. So they spoke to the king of Assyria, saying, The nations whom you have carried away into exile in the cities of Samaria do not know the custom of the god of the land; so he has sent lions among them, and behold, they kill them because they do not know the custom of the god of the land. Then the king of Assyria commanded, saying, Take there one of the priests whom you carried into exile and let him go and live there; and let him teach them the custom of the god of the land. So one of the priests whom they had carried away into exile from Samaria came and lived at Bethel, and taught them how to fear the LORD. But every nation still made gods of its own and put them in the houses of the high place which the people of Samaria had made, every nation in their cities in which they lived" (II Kings 17: 22-29 NASB).

This group of people became the Samaritans of Jesus' day.

Judah & Assyria

In Judah, there were good kings and bad kings. Some kings served the Lord and others did not. Ahaz did not serve the Lord. King Ahaz of Judah even sacrificed one of his sons to an idol. When the kings of Aram and Israel attacked Judah, King Ahaz sent to Assyria for help.

Not only did King Ahaz of Judah not cry out to the Lord and seek help from a pagan ruler, he actually gave treasures from the temple to King Tiglath-pileser as a gift. This greatly angered the LORD. (II Kings 16:7-18) But Assyria didn't stop trying to conquer Jerusalem.

"Now in the fourteenth year of King Hezekiah, Sennacherib king of Assyria came up against all the fortified cities of Judah and seized them. Then Hezekiah king of Judah sent to the king of Assyria at Lachish, saying 'I have done wrong. Withdraw from me; whatever you impose on me I will bear.'" (II Kings 18: 13-14 NASB).

So Hezekiah took gold and silver from God's temple to pacify Sennacherib, but that wasn't enough for the Assyrian king. He sent his army to Jerusalem anyway and the Assyrian leaders called out to Hezekiah, the leaders of Jerusalem, and all the people in Jerusalem to surrender so that they would be treated well. The Assyrian leaders also mocked God's ability to save them and called Hezekiah a liar. Hezekiah told the people to ignore the Assyrian threats and the Jews obeyed.

Hezekiah was scared, but the prophet *"Isaiah said to them, 'Thus you shall say to your master, "Thus says the LORD, 'Do not be afraid because of the words that you have heard, with which the servants of the king of Assyria have blasphemed Me. Behold I will put a spirit in him so that he will hear a rumor and return to his own land. And I will make him fall by the sword in his own land.'"'"* (II Kings 19:6-7 NASB).

Hezekiah prayed to the Lord about this terrible situation and God heard his prayer. Isaiah gave another prophetic word to stir up their faith and let them know that he would take care of their problem.

"Then it happened that night that the angel of the LORD went out and struck 185,000 in the camp of the Assyrians; and when men rose early in the morning, behold, all of them were dead. So Sennacherib king of Assyria departed and returned home and lived at Nineveh. It came about as he was worshipping in the house of Nisroch his god, that Adrammelech and Sharezer killed him with the sword; and they escaped into the land of Ararat. And Esarhaddon his son became king in his place" (II Kings 19: 35-37 NASB).

Assyrian Culture & Religion

Looking back at the Assyrians, we have to be repulsed by their cruelty and brutality, but we can also be impressed by their culture. Cities that surrendered without a fight were absorbed into the empire. Cities that tried to defend themselves were destroyed. Each Assyrian soldier had a lance, a sling, and a bow. Their armor was a pointed helmet and a long leather robe. Soldiers had assistants who carried their shields for them. War was glorified in Assyrian culture.

Just as people collect books today, wealthy Assyrians collected large collections of tablets (their books). King Ashurbanipal, who ruled the Assyrian Empire from Nineveh, was a former scribe. He collected 20,000 tablets that we know of. Maybe he had more tablets.

Gilgamesh was considered to be the direct ancestor of King Sargon who was the father of King Sennacherib. One of the favorite pastimes of Assyrian kings was hunting lions.

"Bull men" (huge carved stone bulls with human heads, beards, hats, five legs, and wings) guarded ancient Assyrian palace entrances. These "bull men" were believed by the Assyrians to be friendly little demons that protected the kings.

The Assyrian religion was dark and scary. Ashur, the chief god was originally the sun god and he demanded a steady diet of executed prisoners of war. Demons who wanted to harm mankind dominated their belief system. Their ghoulish worship rituals are very similar to the Aztec religion. Assyrians believed that they were surrounded all the time by thousands of demons. They tried to appease them so they would not be harmed. If a demon entered someone's body, it was believed to cause disease or death. A ritual with sheep livers was believed to help them foretell the future.

Assyrians had locks and keys to protect their property from intruders and thieves. Inside their locked homes, walls were painted white with a red band near the floor across the walls. Brightly colored rugs adorned the floors. Their homes were built around a central courtyard and they spent most of their time outside in the courtyard.

Assyrian men and women dressed more modestly than their Egyptian and Babylonian neighbors with long robes that covered their entire torso. Clothing was made of brightly colored linen or cotton. Men were very proud of their long beards and mustaches that curled down from their faces. In murals, it looks like Assyrian men wore mullets, a popular haircut in American in the 1980s.

Assyrian sculptors created many statues across the empire. I saw several in the British museum. Another Assyrian art form I really enjoyed was reliefs, or raised carved scenes on a flat surface. Many battles and historical events were memorialized in reliefs.

Babylon

Babylon was a small city-state that was part of the ancient Akkadian Empire. Centuries later, the now independent city-state of Babylon remembered their prestige during the reign of Hammurabi who created a Babylonian Empire that existed only during his lifetime. After this, Babylon found itself part of the Assyrian, Kassite, and Elamite dominions at one time or another. They were very proud of their heritage and grew nostalgic for the old ways of centuries earlier. They even had their own archaeology digs to discover old sites important to their history as Babylonians. They even resurrected the practice of appointing a royal princess to serve as a priestess of the moon-god Sin.

The Assyrians and Babylonians engaged in a power struggle for centuries, but the tide eventually turned in favor of the Babylonians. Joining the Medes, Persians, and other peoples, they sacked Nineveh in 612 B.C.

Babylon was a thriving empire. The center of every city was the temple where idol-gods were worshipped. Each city had local autonomy with laws, courts, and decision-making assemblies. Irrigation systems were build to create large farms and ranches.

Babylonian artists created beautiful murals in royal palaces throughout the Babylonian Empire. In these realistic murals, beings from the spirit world are portrayed as influencing kings and government leaders in a variety of situations. Murals were painted on dry walls. As time went on, frescos began to appear. Like murals, frescoes were painted on wet plaster walls before the plaster dried. The paint and plaster dried together, causing the paint to last longer.

Some of the most famous creations of Babylon are the Hanging Gardens and the Ishtar Gate.

Babylonian Captivity

Nebuchadnezzar II was a great builder. He rebuilt all of Babylon's major cities on a much more lavish scale. His own city, Babylon, was surrounded by a moat and a double circuit of walls. The Euphrates River flowed through the center of the city with a beautiful stone bridge crossing it. In the very center of Babylon was a ziggurat, or temple where their idol-gods were worshipped. The city was considered impenetrable. But God is bigger than any walls or moats.

Nebuchadnezzar II forced tribute from Syria, Phoenicia, Damascus, Tyre, and Sidon. He also attacked and conquered Jerusalem, deposing King Jehoiachin and occupying the city. While Babylon was busy fighting the Egyptians, Jewish King Zedekiah revolted, but after an 18 month long siege, Jerusalem was captured in 587 B.C. and thousands of Jews were deported to Babylon, including Daniel, Shadrach, Meshach, and Abednego. This is called the Babylonian Captivity, a punishment for the sins that the nation of Judah committed against the LORD. Read Daniel to learn more about the adventures of some heroic, godly young men who were taken to Babylon during the Babylonian Captivity.

One night, years later, Belshazzar, the current ruler of Babylon was enjoying a drunken feast with his friends. He called for the Jewish temple gold and silver vessels to be brought out. He and his friends drank from them, while worshipping their pagan-gods to mock the God of Israel.

"Suddenly the fingers of a man's hand emerged and began writing opposite the lampstand on the plaster of the wall of the king's palace, and the king saw the back of the hand that did the writing. Then the king's face grew pale and his thoughts alarmed him, and his hip joints went slack and his knees began knocking together" (Daniel 5: 5-6 NASB).

The king, scared to death, asked for all his diviners and magicians to interpret the words written on the walls, but no one could. Finally his queen reminded him of Daniel. Daniel was brought in and offered riches and gifts if he could interpret the writing on the wall. He told the king to keep his gifts, but did interpret the writing, after first reminding the king of his ancestor's experience with the God of Israel.

"Now this is the inscription that was written out: MENE, MENE, TEKEL, UPHARSIN. This is the interpretation of the message. MENE—God has numbered your kingdom and put an end to it. TEKEL—you have been weighed on the scales and found deficient. PERES—your kingdom has been divided and given over to the Medes and Persians. Then Belshazzar gave orders, and they clothed Daniel with purple and put a necklace of gold around his neck, and issued a proclamation concerning his that he now had authority as the third ruler in the kingdom. That same night Belshazzar, the Chaldean king was slain. So Darius the Mede received the kingdom at about the age of sixty-two" (Daniel 5:25-31 NASB).

You see, Cyrus invaded Babylonia that very night. He had his engineers divert the Euphrates River and the Mede-Persian Army entered the city under the walls through an empty moat. So much for a city that can mock the LORD.

Cyrus allowed the Jews to go back to Jerusalem, but that's another story.

Babylonian Religion

Babylonians did not worship the True God. Instead, they worshipped a wide variety of pagan idols very similar to the Sumerian pantheon. A pantheon is a collection of gods and goddesses worshipped by a people group. Marduk (Sumerian Enlil) was their most powerful god. Shamash (Sumerian Utu) was the god of the sun, Sin (Sumerian Nanna) the moon goddess, Ea (Sumerian Enki) god of the water, and Ishtar (Sumerian Inanna) goddess of love.

Assyrian Food

Flat barley bread was the main staple of the Assyrian diet, eaten at every meal. Pork, mutton, beef, duck, goose, lentils, cucumbers, olives, garlic, onion, lettuce, turnips, goat's milk, and cow's milk were part of their diet. They drank a beverage made of barley.

Babylonian Food

The Babylonian diet was rich and varied. They ate beef, mutton, lamb, goat, pig, deer, chickens, duck, goose, eggs, fish, shellfish, and turtles. In addition, they enjoyed peas, lettuce, beans, cucumbers, cabbage, shallots, leeks, lentils, beats, onions, carrot leaves, and unleavened bread. Fruits were popular and abundant including figs, quinces, mulberries, pomegranates, dates, grapes, peaches, plums, cherries, melons, apricots, pears, and apples. They liked to spice things up with mint, saffron, tarragon, pepper, and salt. They loved to pickle fruits and vegetables using vinegar. Vinegar and oil were mixed to create salad dressings.

Babylonian stew ingredients included honey, mutton fat, and meat juice (the blood of the animal). This is one reason that Daniel and his friends did not want to eat the Babylonian food—eating the blood of an animal was considered unclean.

Ezekiel Bread

2 ½ Cups Wheat Berries

1 ½ Cups Spelt Flour

½ Cup Barley

½ Cup Millet

¼ Cups Dry Green Lentils

2 Tbsp. Dry Great Northern Beans

2 Tbsp. Dry Kidney Beans

2 Tbsp. Dried Pinto Beans

4 Cups Warm Water (110 degrees F/45 degrees C)

1 Cup Honey

1/2 Cup Olive Oil

2 (.25 ounce) Packages Active Dry Yeast

2 Tbsp. Salt

Measure the water, honey, olive oil, and yeast into a large bowl. Let it sit for 3 to 5 minutes. Stir all of the grains and beans together until well mixed. Grind in a flour mill. Add fresh milled flour and salt to the yeast mixture; stir until well mixed, about 10 minutes. The dough will be like that of a batter bread. Pour dough into two greased 9 x 5 inch loaf pans.

Let rise in a warm place for about 1 hour, or until dough has reached the top of the pan. Bake at 350°F (175 degrees C) for 45 to 50 minutes, or until loaves are golden brown.

Nahum's Challah Bread

Challah bread is used to celebrate the Sabbath and many Jewish festivals. It is a lovely braided bread.

1 ½ Cups Warm Water

½ Cups Honey

1 Tbsp. Oil

4 Eggs

1 ½ teaspoons Salt

1 Tbsp. Sugar

2 Tbsp. Active Dry Yeast

5 Cups Flour, plus additional flour (may take 8 or 9 cups of flour total)

Sesame Seeds or Poppy Seeds

Place yeast, sugar and ½ cup water in a small bowl, stir, and let sit until it is foamy. Combine ingredients in a large bowl in order listed. Add enough flour and knead to make a smooth dough. Knead for approximately 10 minutes. Oil top of bread and cover. Let rise in a warm place until almost doubled. Punch down.

Divide dough into 8 pieces. Roll each piece into a rope about 14-15" long and an inch in diameter. Lay 4 ropes side-by-side and pinch tops together. Braid tightly starting on the left, taking the rope over two and under one. Pinch bottom ends and fold under. Place braids on greased baking sheets and cover. Let rise in a warm place for 25-30 minutes.

Brush with beaten eggs and sprinkle with sesame or poppy seeds. Bake at 325 degrees for 30-40 minutes, until done. (If loaves are on two separate sheets, rotate halfway through baking time for even baking.) If loaves start to brown too quickly, loosely lay a piece of foil on top. Cool on wire racks, covered.

Ezekiel Bread II

1 Cup Lentils

2 (.25 ounce) Packages Active Dry Yeast

5 Cups Warm Water (110 degrees F/45 degrees C), divided

5 Tbsp. Olive Oil

1 Tbsp. Salt

1 Tbsp. Honey

8 Cups Whole Wheat Flour

4 Cups Barley Flour

2 Cups Soy Flour

½ Cup Millet Flour

1/4 Cup Rye Flour

Place lentils in a small saucepan, cover with water and cook until soft. Drain and set aside to cool. In a small bowl, dissolve yeast in 1/2 cup warm water. Let stand until creamy, about 10 minutes.

Place the cooled lentils in a bowl and mash. Mix in olive oil, honey, salt and remaining 4 1/2 cups warm water. In a large bowl, mix together whole wheat flour, barley flour, soy flour, millet flour and rye flour.

Stir the yeast mixture into the lentil mixture. Beat in 2 cups of the flour mixture. Stir in the remaining flour mixture, 1 cup at a time, beating well after each addition. When the dough has pulled together, turn it out onto a lightly floured surface and knead until smooth, about 8 minutes. Lightly oil a large bowl, place the dough in the bowl and turn to coat with oil. Cover with a damp cloth and let rise in a warm place until doubled in volume, about 1 hour.

Deflate the dough and turn it out onto a lightly floured surface. Briefly knead the dough and divide into four equal pieces and form into loaves. Place the loaves into four lightly greased 9x5 inch loaf pans. Cover the loaves with a damp cloth and let rise until doubled in volume, about 40 minutes. Meanwhile, preheat oven to 375°F (190° C).

Bake in preheated oven for about 1 hour, or until bottom of a loaf sounds hollow when tapped.

Passover: The Seder Plate

Exodus 11-12

The special foods eaten at Passover are symbolic. The Seder plate has six food items on it, arranged in a special order. The plate is placed on top of the covering of the 3 Matzo in front of the head of the household. Here are the foods.

The Shank Bone

A piece of roasting lamb represents the lamb that was sacrificed and on the Eve of the Exodus, whose blood marked the doorposts of the Israelites, allowing the Angel of Death to "pass over."

The Hard-boiled Egg

The hard-boiled egg represents mourning. The Jews mourn the loss of their temple. But, my favorite is this: The hard boiled egg represents the suffering of the Jews in Egypt under cruel taskmasters. Most things soften when boiled in water, but the egg gets hard. In the same way, the Israelites became stronger because of their suffering.

The Bitter Herbs

Bitter herbs remind us of the bitterness of the slavery of our forefathers in Egypt. People often used grated horseradish, romaine lettuce, or endive.

The Paste (Charoset)

This mixture of apples and nuts resembles the mortar and brick made by the Jewish slaves for Pharoh.

The Vegetable

A non-bitter root vegetable represents the back-breaking work of the Jewish salves. A peeled onion or boiled potato is a common choice.

The Lettuce

The lettuce symbolizes the bitter enslavement of our fathers in Egypt. The leaves of Romaine lettuce are not bitter, but the stem, left to grow in the ground, turns hard and bitter.

Charoset

1 Cup Almonds

1 Cup Pecans

1 Cup Golden raisins

1 Cup Black raisins

1 Cup dried Apricots

1Cup Dates

1 tsp. Apple Pie Spice

1 Cup Grape Juice

Put all ingredients in the food processor until well blended.

Passover Matzo Ball Soup

1 Chicken

2 Whole Onions

4 Stalks Celery, diced

4 Carrots, sliced

Parsley

Salt & Pepper

Add chicken to 2 1/2 quarts cold water, bring to boil and skim. Cook for ½ hour then add vegetables and season. Cook 1 to 1 ½ hours until chicken is tender, then add matzo meal balls.

Matzo Balls

3/4 Cup Matzo Meal

3 Eggs

Separate eggs. Beat yolks and set aside. Beat egg whites until stiff. Fold together, then fold into matzo meal. Salt and pepper and place in refrigerator for 15 minutes. Use hands and form small balls of matzo meal and drop in boiling soup for 25 minutes.

Passover Almond Macaroons

2 Cups Almonds, use up to 1/2 cup more to get a thick enough batter

1 ½ Cups Sugar

3 Egg Whites

1 tsp. Pure Vanilla Extract

Preheat oven to 400°F. Cover two heavy aluminum cookie sheets with parchment paper.

Put the almonds and sugar in the work bowl of a food processor fitted with the metal blade. Process just until the mixture is smooth. Don't over-process! Immediately add the egg whites, before the almonds lose their oil. Pulse about 10 times. Add the vanilla and pulse 2 or 3 times.

You should be able to just shape the batter with your hands. The batter should be sticky and quite thick, like rough, sticky clay. The size of the eggs used and the amount of oil in the almonds determines the consistency, so be prepared to add a bit more almonds or egg white.

Shape the batter into balls the size of walnuts. Arrange on the parchment covered baking sheets. Brush each macaroon with a bit of water. Bake for 16 minutes, or until lightly brown. Remove the cookie sheets from the oven, cool on the parchment, on racks. Cool completely and store, tightly covered, at room temperature for a week. These freeze very well.

Shadrach's Veggie Crescent Roll Squares

2 (8 ounce) Packages Refrigerated Crescent Rolls

2 (8 ounce) Packages Cream Cheese, softened

1 Cup Mayonnaise

1 (1 ounce) package dry Ranch-style dressing mix

1 Cup Fresh Broccoli, chopped

1 Cup Tomatoes, chopped

1 Cup Green Bell Pepper, chopped

1 Cup Cauliflower, chopped

1 Cup Carrots, shredded

1 Cup Cheddar Cheese, shredded

Preheat oven to 375 degrees F (190 degrees C). Roll out the crescent roll dough onto a 9x13 inch baking sheet, and pinch together edges to form a crust.

Bake crust for 12 minutes in the preheated oven. Once finished cooking, remove crust from oven and let cool 15 minutes without removing it from the baking sheet.

In a small mixing bowl, combine cream cheese, mayonnaise, and dry Ranch dressing. Spread the mixture over the cooled crust. Arrange broccoli, tomato, green bell pepper, cauliflower, shredded carrots, and Cheddar cheese over the cream cheese layer. Chill for one hour, slice and serve.

Daniel's Veggie Bagel Pizza

1 Whole Wheat or Whole Grain Bagel, cut in half

Tomato Sauce or Pizza Sauce

Grated Mozzarella Cheese

Red Pepper, chopped finely

Green Pepper, chopped finely

Onion, chopped finely

Olives, sliced and pitted

Oregano

Basil

Preheat oven to 350°. Place bagel halves on greased cookie sheet. Spread tomato sauce onto each half- bagel. Add toppings and cover with cheese. Sprinkle with oregano and basil. Bake in oven until cheese is bubbling.

King Josiah's Roasted Chicken

4 Tbsp. Olive Oil

1 Whole Chicken

Salt

Pepper

Garlic Powder

Onion Powder

Italian Seasoning

Place the chicken in a greased pan breast side up. Rub with olive oil. Sprinkle with spices generously. Bake @ 350° for 2 hours or until finished.

Fig Newtons

FOR DOUGH

3 Cup Flour shopping list

1/2 Cup Sugar

1/2 tsp. Salt shopping list

3/4 tsp. Baking Powdershopping list

3/8 tsp. Baking Soda shopping list

1/2 tsp. Cinnamonshopping list

12 Tbsp. (1 ½ Stick) Butter, room temperature, cut in piecesshopping list

4 Eggs, separated

FOR FILLING

2 Cups Figs, chopped or dried shopping list

1 Cup Orange Juiceshopping list

1 Cup Apple Juice shopping list

½ tsp Cinnamon shopping list

4 Tbsp. Sugarshopping list

1 tsp. Orange Peel or Zest of 1 Orange shopping list

FOR DOUGH

Combine the dry ingredients in a large bowl. Using a pastry blender, cut in butter pieces until the dough is sandy looking. Whisk 3 eggs together and add to the dough. Mix to combine. Form the dough into a ball, wrap in plastic and refrigerate for 2 hours.

FOR FILLING

Combine all the filling ingredients in a saucepan or skillet and cook over medium heat until all the liquid is absorbed by the figs and the mixture is thick. Stir during cooking. Let the filling cool slightly, then puree in a food processor until smooth. Refrigerate until ready to bake.

For an easier version, sub the filling with 2 cups of fig preserves. When ready to bake, heat the oven to 375F. Make an egg wash by whisking the remaining egg with 2 tsp. of water.

Zephaniah's Pistachio Dessert

2 Cups Milk

2 Packages Pistachio Instant Pudding

1 Can Crushed Pineapple, drained

2 Cups Miniature Marshmallows

1 Cup Pecans, chopped

1 Container Cool Whip

Mix pudding with milk. Add pineapple, marshmallows, and pecans. Fold in whipped topping. Pour into serving bowl, cover, and refrigerator.

Hanging Garden Date Nut Bread

2 ½ Dates, chopped

¼ Cup Butter

1 Cup Boiling Water

½ Cup Brown Sugar, packed

1 Egg

1 Cup Almonds, chopped

Preheat the oven to 350 degrees F (175 degrees F). Grease and flour a 9x5 inch loaf pan. In a medium bowl, combine the dates and butter. Pour boiling water over them, and let stand until cool.

When the dates have cooled, stir the mixture to break up any clumps. Mix in the brown sugar and egg until well blended. Combine the flour, baking soda, baking powder, and salt; stir into the date mixture until just blended. Pour into the prepared pan.

Bake for 50 minutes in the preheated oven, or until a wooden pick inserted into the center comes out clean.

Israel, Assyrians, & Babylonians Reading & Listening

The Mystery of History Volume I: Creation to the Resurrection by Linda Lacour Hobar (Bright Ideas Press) Chapters 1-3

Ancient Civilizations & The Bible by Diana Waring (Answers in Genesis) Unit 1

Streams of Civilization Volume I by Mary Stanton & Albert Hyma (Christian Liberty Press) Introductions & Chapter 1

History of the World in Christian Perspective by Jerry H. Combee (A'Beka Book) Chapter 1

The Usborne Story of Music by Simon Mundy (Usborne Publishing)

The Usborne Story of Painting by Anthea Peppin (Usborne Publishing)

The Usborne Book of Living Long Ago: Everyday Life Through the Ages By Felicity Brooks and Helen Edom (Usborne Publishing)

God King by Joanne Williamson (Bethlehem Books)

Sinbad's Seven Voyages retold by Gladys Davidson (Scholastic)

Audio CDs

What in the World is Going on Here? Volume 1: Ancient Civilizations and the Bible Disc 3 Track 1-4

Digger Deeper Volume 1: Ancient Civilizations and the Bible Disc 2 Track 3

Movies

Veggie Tales: Jonah (Illustra Media)

Israel, Assyrians, & Babylonians Menu

Lunch

Ezekiel Bread

Beef Barley Soup

Fig Newtons

Lunch

Hezekiah Celebrates the Passover with a Seder Plate

Charoset

Matzo Ball Soup

Almond Macaroons

Lunch

Nahum's Challah Bread

King Josiah's Roasted Chicken

Zephaniah Pistachio Pudding Dessert

Lunch

Shadrach's Veggie Crescent Roll Squares

Daniel's Veggie Bagel Pizza

Hanging Gardens Date Nut Bread

Ancient China & India

China

China has been inhabited since God scattered people from the Tower of Babel. The early Chinese made silk from silkworms, creating beautiful clothing. They made pottery on a potter's wheel and baked bricks to use for building. Building dykes to control flooding, the Chinese showed themselves to be engineers. They also created irrigation systems for their farms. A feudal system existed where one family oversaw a large tract of land employing many peasants to work the land.

The Chinese people had chariots for transportation. They were great archers and loved to throw hunting parties. Bronze candlesticks and jade carvings were popular. Chinese writing was a kind of pictographs with each word represented by a pictograph. Writing became an art form in China through calligraphy.

China under Shang & Chou Dynasties

The first Chinese ruling family, the Shang dynasty, ruled for 600 years, followed by the Chou (or Zhou) dynasty that ruled for 800 years. The people of China believed that the rulers had a "Mandate from Heaven" to rule the people. You see when the Chou dynasty wanted to take over from the Shang dynasty, they told everyone that the "gods" had decided that the Shang's time was over because they were so selfish. It was time for the Chou dynasty. The ruler felt that he was chosen by the "gods" and therefore had religious power. The ruler was expected to care about the Chinese people and not be selfish.

During these years, art was produced, the economy flourished, and literature was written. The Chinese people made beautiful painted tiles. Roads were built and people traveled from place to place. The Chinese loved astronomy and growing flowers in little gardens. Each Chinese city was protected by a large thick wall. I am talking a big wall. A wall might be 30 feet high, 65 feet across, and miles long.

The peasants wore tunics and trousers, while the richer folk wore fancy silk clothing.

Family was very important to the Chinese people. The oldest man was the head of the family. Wives became part of the husband's family, while daughters became part of the family they married into. Children were expected to be respectful and obedient. Arguing was considered shameful. If anyone in a family did something wrong, the whole family suffered disgrace.

Warriors fought in chariots, on horseback, or on foot. Armor was made of bronze. Soldiers carried metal daggers, spears, and axes.

China under the Qin & Han Dynasties

Qin united all of what we know as China today under his own rule. He only ruled for 15 years, dying of natural causes, but he created what we know as "China". Qin developed a system of bureaucracy so that he could keep tight control over all of his subjects. He divided his empire into 36 provinces and put two government officials in charge of each province. They were supposed to keep an eye on each other. The provinces were divided up into districts and each district had two people in charge.

Qin also decided to build a huge wall to protect China from foreign invaders. He also built bridges, roads, and canals. He created a law that applied to every citizen. No one was above the law.

When Qin died, his son took the throne, but a peasant revolt usurped the throne and so the Han dynasty began.

During the Han years, paper was invented and things began to be written down. Pottery, jewelry, book covers, and ornaments were created that were delicate and lovely. Paper lanterns became popular. Pottery was decorated with illustrations of dragons, trees, and people. Education was encouraged. The "Silk Road," or trade route between the Roman Empire and China, brought wealth of gold, silver, and precious jewels into China because the Romans wanted Chinese silk.

Confucius spent many years traveling with a nobleman while working on his education. He tried to learn everything he could learn and became a teacher. Confucius came to believe that everything had to be done a certain way and wrote down strict rules for every imaginable situation. The nobles and leaders liked his rules and soon his philosophy of living was embraced with religious zeal. His teachings remained popular for centuries.

Chinese Food

The Chinese ate with chopsticks and enjoyed spices to flavor their food. Rice was one of the earliest grains farmers grew. People cooked rice with boiling water just like they do today. People in northern China grew millet and sorghum instead of rice. Millet was boiled into a porridge. Tea was also very popular from the earliest days in China. Wheat and soybeans were also staples. Vegetables were eaten with their rice and bread and included cucumbers and bok choy. The Chinese ate chicken, pork, mutton, and beef. They enjoyed citrons, peaches, and apricots. Spices such as ginger and anise were very popular.

India

Another civilization grew up along the Indus River. These people had a complicated writing system called Indus Script with 400-600 different written symbols. These symbols were pressed into clay with seals, or stamps. They built huge cities with wells, drainage systems, and roads laid out in a square grid. Farmers lived outside the cities and grew melons, wheat, peas, dates, sesame seeds, and cotton.

Indo-European people migrated to India from an area between the Black Sea and the Caspian Sea. They brought their language, Sanskrit with them, as well as horses and the Hindu religion.

About this time, the Indian caste system got started. This horrible way of life was a permanent division of people into different groups, or castes. There were four castes with one category below the four castes called the untouchables. The untouchables had the worst jobs and were avoided by everyone else. The lowest caste was the Sudras, made up of servants and employees. The caste above the Sudras, was the Vaisyas, business owners and farmers. The next caste was the Kshatriyas, or warriors. The highest caste was the Brahmins who were the religious priests. Within each caste were several different categories each with different levels. People from different castes could not eat together, marry, or build friendships with one another.

This group of people in the Indus River Valley eventually became sixteen different kingdoms. During that time, a prince named Siddhartha Gautama decided to give up his title and search for truth. He became known as "Buddha", or the "enlightened one." While Shadrach, Meshach, and Abednego were living in Babylon as exiles from Israel, Buddha was teaching his "way of enlightenment" that would enslave millions of people. Buddhism spread to China, Japan, and Southeast Asia.

Indian Food

Rice and bread (wheat) were main staples in the Indian diet, along with chickpeas, lentils, beef, pork, mutton, goat, and chicken. Spices like cinnamon, cumin, coriander, anise, and fennel were used to flavor stews, soups, and other meals. Sugar cane grew plentifully in India and was a favorite treat!

When the Hindus began to worship "mother goddess," they believed that cows were sacred to her, and so Hindus stopped eating beef. At that time, the Indians learned to make sugar cubes.

China: Honey Glazed Chicken Wings

12 Chicken Wings

½ Cup Soy Sauce

½ Cup Water

½ Cup Honey

2 Cloves Garlic, crushed

1 Tbsp. Ginger

In a large greased baking pan, mix soy sauce, water, honey, garlic and ginger. Toss chicken wings in the mixture to coat thoroughly. Let wings marinate for 2 hours. Broil wings for 10 minutes each side.

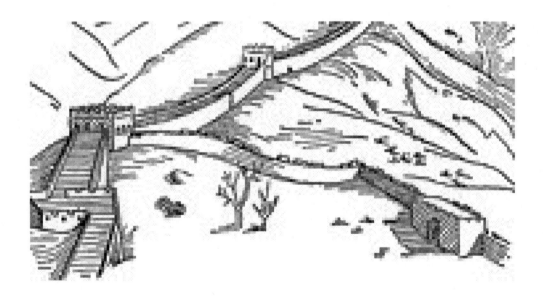

India: Chicken Curry

1 Tbsp. Oil

1 Onion, chopped

1 Boneless, Skinless Chicken Breast, cut into chunks

2 Tbsp. Butter

2 Tbsp. Curry Powder

1 Clove Garlic, crushed

1 Cup Coconut Milk (can substitute 1 cup plain yogurt)

½ Cup Golden Raisins

½ Cup Frozen Peas

Sauté chicken and onion in oil. Melt butter in another frying pan, add curry and garlic. Cook for 3 minutes. Stir in coconut milk and raisins. Add chicken and onion to pan. Cover and simmer for 25 minutes. Add peas during last five minutes.

Serve with Basmati rice.

Condiments: Set out little bowls filled with golden raisins, chopped peanuts, chopped cashew nuts, plain yogurt and chutney. Everyone can top their curry with their favorite condiments.

Han Chinese Pepper Steak

1 ½ lb. Top Round Steak

2 Tbsp. Vegetable Oil

1 Clove Garlic, minced

1 tsp. Salt

1 Cup Beef Broth

1 Cup Julienned Bell Pepper

1 Cup Thinly Sliced Celery

¼ Cup Thinly Sliced Onion

½ Cup Coca-Cola

2 Medium Ripe Tomatoes

2 ½ Tbsp. Cornstarch

¼ Cup Coca-Cola

1 Tbsp. Soy Sauce

Hot Cooked Rice

Trim all fat from the meat and cut into pencil thin strips. In a deep skillet or Dutch oven, heat oil, garlic, and salt. Add the meat and brown over high heat, about 10 minutes, stirring occasionally with a fork.

Add the beef broth. Cover and simmer for 15 to 20 minutes, or until the meat is fork-tender. Stir in the green pepper strips, celery, onions and 1/2 cup Coca-Cola. Cover and simmer for 5 minutes.

Do not overcook; the vegetables should be crisp-tender. Peel the tomatoes; cut into wedges and gently stir into meat mixture. Blend cornstarch with 1/4 cup of Coca-Cola and the soy sauce. Stir into the meat mixture until the sauce thickens, about 1 minute, stirring lightly with a fork. Serve over hot rice.

Indus River Fried Barley

2 Cups Pearl Barley

Cooking Spray

2 Eggs, lightly beaten

½ Cup Water

2 tsp. Sesame Oil

3 Scallions, sliced

½ lb. Bacon

1 Stalk Celery

1 Red Pepper, diced

1 Carrot, diced

1 Cup Peas

½ lb. Broccoli, chopped

2 Tbsp. Soy Sauce

1 Tbsp. Sweet Chili Sauce

Cook barley in large pan of boiling water for 40 minutes or until soft. Drain and set aside.

Lightly spray a wok and heat up to medium heat. Whisk together eggs and 2 Tbsp. water and cook in wok. Remove omelet and slice into strips; set aside. Heat oil in wok and fry bacon and onions. Add celery, pepper, carrot, and remaining water; stir fry for 5 minutes. Add peas and broccoli; cook until tender. Stir in barley, soy sauce, and chili sauce; heat through. Fold in omelet slices and serve warm.

India: EZ Fruity Macaroons

4 Cups Flaked Coconut

1 Can (14 oz) Sweetened Condensed Milk

½ tsp. Almond Extract

1 Package (3 oz.) Strawberry or Cherry Gelatin

In large bowl, combine all ingredients and mix thoroughly. Cover and refrigerate at least 2 hours. Spoon into 1" balls and bake at 350 for 8-10 minutes

Indus Valley Spiced Chai Tea

Tea was imported from China, but the Indians spiced it up and made it their own.

1 Stick Cinnamon

4 Cardamom Seeds

4 Cloves

3 Cups Water

1 Cups Heavy Cream

1 Tbsp. Honey

2 tsp. Strong Black Tea

Put cinnamon, cardamom seeds, and cloves in water and bring to a boil. Turn down to low and let simmer for 5 minutes. Add cream honey, back tea, and bring to a boil again.

India & China Reading & Listening

The Mystery of History Volume I: Creation to the Resurrection by Linda Lacour Hobar (Bright Ideas Press) Chapters 1-3

Ancient Civilizations & The Bible by Diana Waring (Answers in Genesis) Unit 1

Streams of Civilization Volume I by Mary Stanton & Albert Hyma (Christian Liberty Press) Introductions & Chapter 1

History of the World in Christian Perspective by Jerry H. Combee (A'Beka Book) Chapter 1

A Grain of Rice by Helena Clare Pittman (Yearling)

Adventures in Ancient China by Linda Bailey (Kids Can Press)

Audio CDs

What in the World is Going on Here? Volume 1: Ancient Civilizations and the Bible Disc 3 Track 5-7

Digger Deeper Volume 1: Ancient Civilizations and the Bible Disc 2 Track 4-5

India & China Menu

Lunch

Han Chinese Pepper Steak

Rice

India EZ Fruity Macaroons

Lunch

India Chicken Curry with Rice

Spiced Chai Tea

Lunch

China Honey Glazed Chicken Wings

Fried Barley

Persians & Medes

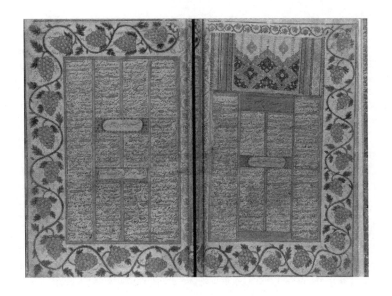

Media & Persia

The Medes, a combination of tribes united under King Deioces, lived in present-day Iran and included the city of Laodicia. The Magi, a special caste that ministered to the spiritual needs of their people, were Medes. This role was hereditary and passed from father to son.

The Medes spend time under Assyria's rule and were brought into the Persian Empire by Cyrus the Great. Not much is known about the Medes and mention of them is usually as part of the Persians.

Persians were nomads who lived in the area of present-day Iran. Eventually they found themselves under the rule of the Medes. Cyrus the Great led a revolt against Media and went on to conquer Lydia and Babylon. Cyrus the Great is considered the founder of the first Persian Empire. He was a famous builder and able administrator. His kingdom was the largest of all the ancient empires. At one point it spanned from the Balkan Mountains to the Indus Valley (under Darius the Great). He built roads, had a mail system, declared an official language, and set up a strong administration where he gave his conquered peoples autonomy to make decisions, practice their own religion, and enjoy relative freedom. They were able to retain their own culture and laws.

Persian Culture

Here are some interesting things about Persian culture.

Truth was important to the Persians and liars might be executed.

They loved desserts and celebrated birthdays by consuming lots of sweet treats.

The original Persians and Medes were ranchers of cattle and horses.

Persian rugs were beautifully ornate and are still popular today.

The Persians used the Aramaic language for writing, using the Phoenician alphabet, and writing on papyrus.

The Persians did everything in grand style. They constructed beautiful buildings, gardens, and artwork. Murals, Frescoes, statues, pottery, and jewelry were crafted from the finest materials and decorated with gold, silver, ebony, and precious stones. Darius the Great collected artists from all over his vast empire, enjoying a wide variety of artist style and expression.

Queen Esther Saves the Day

King Xerxes threw a party for all his officials in his kingdom for 180 days. For the most part, he wanted to show off all his wealth and glory while feasting and drinking with abandon. When this was over, he held a party for seven days for all the people in Susa from the greatest to the least. Lots of drinking took place. Meanwhile, his wife, Queen Vashti gave a party for the ladies. On the seventh day, the extremely intoxicated king sent for his wife to show off her beauty. She refused to come to be gawked at so he decided to find another queen. He already had many wives.

After a long series of beauty treatments, a lovely Jewish girl named Esther was chosen from among all the virgins in the land. King Xerxes made her his queen.

In time, a leader in the kingdom named Haman developed a dastardly plan to destroy all the Jews in the Persian Empire. After fasting and prayer, Esther pleaded to the king for her life and the life of her people. God used her to protect His people.

Of course there is much more to this exciting adventure and you can read all about it in the book of Esther.

Median & Persian Food

Flatbread was the staple of the Persian diet. Records show that Persians enjoyed all kinds of meat, poultry, vegetables, herbs, seeds, blossoms, and fruits. Just think of all the foods the Sumerians, Egyptians, Israelites, Assyrians, and Babylonians ate and you get an idea of what the Persians ate. They loved dairy products such as milk, cheese, and yogurt. As the empire expanded, more foods were added to create wide variety in the diet. They enjoyed stews, dumplings, kebabs, and stuffed vegetables.

Persians drank wine liberally.

Basil, cloves, cumin, coriander, mint, saffron, and pepper were important spices. Glazes were often added to vegetables and sauces to meat. Sesame seeds, orange peel, raisins, almonds, pistachios, and walnuts were often added to main dishes and desserts.

Persians loved desserts and definitely had a sweet tooth!

Cyrus the Great Almond Stew

2 lb. Beef Stew Meat

1 lb. Almonds, slivered

2 Onions, diced

½ Tbsp. Saffron

4 Tbsp. Oil

4 Tbsp. Tomato Paste

2 Dried Limes

1 Cinnamon Stick

1 Cup Raisins

Salt, Turmeric, & Red Pepper to Taste

Soak saffron in water for 20 minutes. Sauté onions in oil until golden. Garnish with turmeric. Stir in beef and continue frying. Add water to cover beef, cover, and cook for an hour over medium heat. Stir in tomato paste. Add salt and crushed red peppers. Add dried limes, slivered almonds, and cinnamon sticks. Stir thoroughly, cover pot, and boil for 15 minutes. Add saffron and raisins. Remove cinnamon stick. Simmer another 10 minutes. Serve warm.

Darius Green Beans

2 Packages (16 oz. each) frozen green beans

¼ Cup Butter

½ Cup Sliced Almonds

1 Large Onion, chopped

2 Tbsp. Minced Garlic

Salt & Pepper to Taste

Cook & drain green beans according to package directions. In small frying pan, sauté almonds, onions, garlic, salt, & pepper in butter. Mix with green beans and serve hot!

Esther's Jewish Apple Cake

3 Cups Apples, sliced thin

2 tsp. Cinnamon

5-7 Tbsp. Sugar

2 Cups Sugar

1 Cup Corn Oil

4 Eggs

1/3 Cup Orange Juice

3 Cups Flour

3 tsp. Baking Powder

2 ½ tsp. Vanilla

Sprinkle cinnamon and sugar over apples- set aside. Cream sugar and oil. Add eggs, orange juice and vanilla. Sift flour, baking powder add to batter and mix well. Put a layer of batter into a greased pan, and then put in a layer of apples. Alternate until the batter and apples are finished. Bake at 375 F for ½ an hour. Then for a hour at 350 F.

Persians & Medes Reading & Listening

The Mystery of History Volume I: Creation to the Resurrection by Linda Lacour Hobar (Bright Ideas Press) Chapters 1-3

Ancient Civilizations & The Bible by Diana Waring (Answers in Genesis) Unit 1

Streams of Civilization Volume I by Mary Stanton & Albert Hyma (Christian Liberty Press) Introductions & Chapter 1

History of the World in Christian Perspective by Jerry H. Combee (A'Beka Book) Chapter 1

Cyrus the Persian by Sherman A Nagel (A. B. Publishing)

Shadow Spinner by Susan Fletcher (Aladdin Paperbacks)

Within the Palace Gates: The King's Cupbearer by Anna P Siviter (A. B. Publishing)

Hand Me Another Brick by Charles Swindoll (Thomas Nelson)

Audio CDs

What in the World is Going on Here? Volume 1: Ancient Civilizations and the Bible Disc 3 Track 5-7

Digger Deeper Volume 1: Ancient Civilizations and the Bible Disc 2 Track 4-5

Movies

Veggie Tales: Esther

Persians & Medes Menu

Lunch

Cyrus the Great Almond Stew

Darius Green Beans

Esther's Apple Cake

Greece City-States

Early Greece

Ancient Greece was not one nation, but several independent city-states that shared a religion of worshipping idol/gods. Each city was a self-ruling nation. The Greeks flourished in the warm climate and fertile land.

The Trojan War

The Trojan War took place in the twelfth or thirteenth century while the Greek city-states existed, but the Greek culture was in its infancy. Our understanding of the Trojan War comes from two works by Homer, a Greek writer, and one epic poem by Virgil, a Roman writer. Truth was mixed in with mythology. Their idol/gods and idol/goddesses were involved in the battles and underlying goals of the war.

When Paris, a prince of Troy, kidnapped Helen, the Queen of Sparta, the Greek city-states came together to rescue Queen Helen from Troy.

Greek City-States

East of Babylon, Greece was, and still is, a beautiful land made up of two peninsulas and thousands of islands in the Aegean and Ionian Seas. With a warm climate and great soil for growing crops, God blessed them with a long growing season. Greece was not one big country like we think of today. Greece was made up of many city-states that ruled and defended themselves. Each city-state had its own flavor. For example, Spartans lived simple lives, glorified war, and focused completely on raising soldiers to fight victoriously, while Athenians promoted beauty, grace, and philosophizing. All the Greeks did share a common culture, language, and religion. They worshipped many idol-gods who behaved badly.

Very competitive, the Greeks city-states often fought with one another. However once a year, all the Greeks agreed to refrain from fighting long enough to compete with one another in the Olympic Games.

When Persia decided to conquer Greece one city at a time, the city-states came together under the leadership of Athenian generals to protect their freedom. Once they were safe from Persian bullying, Athens, one of the larger Greek city-states, entered her golden years. Art, architecture, music, drama, and writing flourished. It was important to say beautiful things, appreciate beautiful things, and be as beautiful inside and outside as possible. Their sculptures were lifelike.

While Daniel was serving the Lord during the Babylonian Captivity, Aesop was writing his fables that are still enjoyed today.

While Ezra was serving the captives who returned to Jerusalem, Socrates was teaching his disciples Greek philosophy.

Plato was teaching his own disciples in Athens while Malachi was prophesying the Word of the Lord.

The Greek historian, Herodotus, wrote popular histories and is considered the father of history.

One of the things we can thank the Greeks for is their architectural columns

Greek Columns

One of the things we can thank the Greeks for is their architectural columns

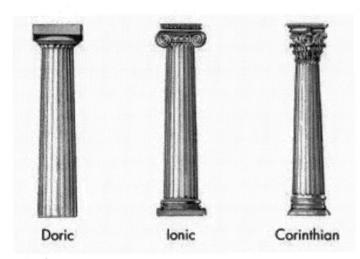

Doric   Ionic   Corinthian

Greek architecture brought us the column. Greek buildings had large decorative columns at the front of their buildings and in their courtyards. There were three types of columns: Doric, Ionic, and Corinthian.

These columns were all over Greece and were adopted by the Romans. Centuries later, in the Renaissance, Greek columns became popular again. Our capitol and Supreme Court building have beautiful Greek columns.

Athens

Athens was named after Athena, the goddess of wisdom and war. In the center of the city, inside the Acropolis, a shrine was built for her. This shrine, the Parthenon was a place for worship and to store gold.

The Acropolis was built on a hill with large thick walls and was used as a fortress when the city was attacked. Beside the Parthenon, the Acropolis was home to several outdoor theatres where plays were performed.

The Agora was the center of business and government with an open area for meetings surrounded by temples to various gods. Elders in the city would come together to discuss issues and make decisions in the Agora. Citizens in Athens could vote for their leaders and vote on laws. When people participate in the choosing and running their government, we call it democracy, or rule by the people.

Greek Clothing

Greek clothing was made of wool (from sheep) and linen (from flax). Some wealthy Greeks had clothing made of imported silk from China. They wore long tunics, usually white, with a long sash. The men's tunic was shorter than the women's tunic. They also wore leather sandals.

Men and women wore rings, necklaces, earrings, and pins. Women wore makeup to make their skins pale, as well as lipstick. Men and women oiled and perfumed their hair.

Greek Language

The Greek language spread throughout Eastern Europe, Northern Africa, and Europe and was spoken in Easter Europe for hundreds of years. Many of words have Greek roots. We still use Greek letters in math, science, and engineering equations. College Fraternities and Sororities use Greek letters in their names.

Most importantly, the New Testament was written in Ancient Greek. Pastors and Bible scholars have studied Ancient Greek for centuries so they can study the Bible in its original language.

Alexander the Great

Alexander the Great was the king of Macedonia, a Greek city-state that began to conquer other Greek city-states. Alexander was a mighty soldier and amazing military commander. Ruling all of Greece was not enough for Alexander. He wanted to conquer the entire world. Growing up, Alexander loved to read Homer. Homer's tales of the Iliad and the Odyssey may have inspired Alexander to be a great military hero.

First, Alexander conquered all of Asia Minor (currently Turkey). Next, he defeated the Persians to conquer Syria, and moved on to Tyre. Alexander the Great went on to conquer Egypt, Babylonia, and the entire Persian Empire.

At this point, Alexander the Great had the largest empire in history. Before he could rule his vast empire, he died. His empire was divided up between four of his generals.

As a child, he was tutored by Aristotle, a disciple of Socrates. Alexander was steeped in Greek culture, language, and philosophy. Everywhere he went, he spread Greek culture and language.

Greek Food

The Greeks ate three meals a day. Breakfast was a light meal of bread or porridge. Lunch was another light meal with bread, cheese, and figs. Dinner was the big meal and it was a feast with a variety of food including meat, fish, bread, eggs, vegetables, and cheese.

The Greeks loved fish, but also ate chicken, beef, lamb, and pork. Some of the common foods enjoyed by the Greeks were cucumbers, beans, cabbage, onions, garlic, figs, grapes, apples, and honey. Honeycakes were a special treat. They also ate eels, small birds, locusts, and "black soup." Black soup was made from pig's blood, salt, and vinegar.

Men and women often ate separately. They drank water and wine. An athlete's diet was mostly meat. Bread was used to soak up soup or sauce, or sometimes as a napkin. At dinner banquets, they lied on their sides to eat.

Pythagoras' Garlic Right Triangles

Bread Slices, favorite kind

Butter

Garlic Powder

Butter bread slices and sprinkle garlic powder on each slice. Cut carefully so that each piece is a right triangle. Bake @ 350° until crisp.

Pythagoras' Cinnamon Right Triangles

Bread Slices, favorite kind

Butter

Cinnamon/Sugar mixture

Toast bread, butter, and sprinkle cinnamon/sugar mixture on top. Cut carefully so that each piece is a right triangle.

Greek Leg of Lamb Roast

1 Leg of Lamb (about 5-6 pounds), butterflied

½ Cup Olive Oil

Juice of 1 Lemon

4 Tbsp. Oregano

1 Tbsp. Salt (sea salt is best)

4 Cloves Garlic, crushed

2 extra Lemons, quartered

Parsley

Preheat oven to 425°F degrees. Cut slits in the lamb and poke garlic cloves in slits. Mix oil, lemon, and garlic together and spread over lamb. Rub salt and oregano over lamb. Place lamb in roasting pan, turn heat down to 325°F, and roast for 4 hours. Serve with lemon wedges and parsley sprigs on the side.

Golden Age Gyro Pita Wrap

1 Medium Onion, finely chopped

2 Pounds Ground Lamb

1 Tbsp. Finely Minced Garlic

2 tsp. Kosher Salt

1 Tbsp. Dried Marjoram

½ tsp. Ground Pepper

1 Tbsp. Dried Ground Rosemary

Pita Bread

Lettuce

Feta Cheese

Tomato

Diced Onion

Tzatziki Sauce

Process the onion in a food processor for 10 to 15 seconds and turn out into the center of a tea towel. Gather up the ends of the towel and squeeze until almost all of the juice is removed. Discard juice.

Return the onion to the food processor and add the lamb, garlic, marjoram, rosemary, salt and pepper and process until it is a fine paste, approximately 1 minute. Stop the processor as needed to scrape down sides of bowl.

Preheat oven 325°F. Place mixture in a loaf pan, making sure to press into the sides of the pan. Place the loaf pan into a water bath and bake for 60-75 minutes or until the mixture reaches 165°F to 170°F. Remove from the oven and drain off any fat. Place the loaf pan on a cooling rack and place a brick wrapped in aluminum foil directly on the surface of the meat and allow to sit for 15 to 20 minutes, until the internal temperature reaches 175°F.

Slice and serve on pita bread with tzatziki sauce, chopped onion, tomatoes, lettuce and feta cheese.

Plato's Spanakopita (Greek Spinach Pie)

2 Unbaked Pastry Shells or Phyllo Sheets

1 Pound Spinach

2 Cups Feta Cheese

6 Scallions

1 Bunch Aniseed – finely chopped

2 Tbsp. Fresh Mint – chopped

2 Tbsp. Olive Oil

For the Egg Wash

1 Egg Well Beaten with ½ Cup Milk

Finely chop the spring onions and spinach, put them in a pan with water. Add the mint and aniseed. Bring to the boil, stirring well. Remove from the heat and put the mixture in a colander to drain well. Press the mixture with a spoon in order to remove as much liquid as possible. Transfer the mixture to a bowl.

Crumble the feta cheese and add it to the mixture along with the olive oil. Stir and then set aside.

Spread the filling evenly in pastry shell or spread evenly on top of phyllo sheets and layer. Brush the top or final sheet with olive oil and, then, with a mixture of beaten egg and milk. Bake @ 350°F for about an hour or until a golden color.

Aesop's Lemon Rice Pilaf

2 Tbsp. Oil

2 Tbsp. Butter

1 Large Scallion, finely chopped

2 Cups Long Grain Rice

4 Cups Chicken Broth

2 Tbsp. Fresh Thyme Leaves

Zest from 1 Lemon

½ Cups Parsley, finely chopped

½ Cup Toasted Slivered Almonds for Garnish

Sauté scallions in oil and butter. Add rice and brown the rice for a few minutes, stirring frrequently. Add chicken broth and thyme and bring to a boil. Reduce heat to low, cover and let sit. Add lemon zest and parsley; mix well. Garnish with almonds.

Pericles' Vasilopita

1 Cup Sliced Almonds

1 Cup Butter

2 Cups Sugar

6 Eggs (beat whites first and put them aside)

3 ½ Cups Flour

2 tsp, Baking Powder

1 Cup Milk

SYRUP

1 ½ Cup Sugar

1 ½ Cup Water

½ Lemon

Beat the butter and blend with the sugar. Add egg yolks. Mix in the flour and baking powder. Warm milk and pour into butter mixture. Beat the egg whites until thick and pour into flour mixture. Stir mixture with spatula and blend in the almonds. Spray round baking pan with non stick baking spray and pour mixture into pan.

Bake 350°F for 40 minutes.

Marathon Honey Puffs

1 ½ Cups Flour

3 tsp. Baking Powder

4 Tbsp. Sugar

4 Tbsp. Oil, or melted butter or margarine

3/4 Cups Milk

1 Egg

Oil for frying

Honey for drizzling

Finely chopped Almonds

Ground Cinnamon

Sift the flour with the baking powder into a bowl. Add sugar, oil (or butter or margarine), milk, and the egg, and mix with a wooden spoon until smooth. Heat 1-2 inches of oil in a deep frying pan to just below the smoke point (medium to medium-high on most stoves). When the oil is hot enough, drop the batter by the small teaspoonful into the oil and fry until golden on all sides.

Tip: Keep a small bowl of cold water next to the workspace and dip finger before pushing batter into the oil (to keep batter from sticking). Drain on paper toweling.

Place on serving platter and drizzle with honey. Dust with walnuts and cinnamon, and serve.

Golden Age Baklava

1 Pound Chopped Mixed Nuts

1 tsp. Ground Cinnamon

1 (16 oz.) Package Phyllo Dough

1 Cup Butter, melted

1 Cup Sugar

1 Cup Water

1/2 Cup Honey

1 tsp. Vanilla Extract

1 tsp. Grated Lemon Zest

Preheat oven to 350°F (175°C). Butter a 9x13 inch baking dish. Toss together cinnamon and nuts. Unroll phyllo and cut whole stack in half to fit the dish. Cover phyllo with a damp cloth while assembling the baklava, to keep it from drying out. Place two sheets of phyllo in the bottom of the prepared dish. Brush generously with butter. Sprinkle 2 to 3 tablespoons of the nut mixture on top. Repeat layers until all ingredients are used, ending with about 6 sheets of phyllo. Using a sharp knife, cut baklava (all the way through to the bottom of the dish) into four long rows, then (nine times) diagonally to make 36 diamond shapes.

While baklava is baking, combine sugar and water in a small saucepan over medium heat and bring to a boil. Stir in honey, vanilla and lemon zest, reduce heat and simmer 20 minutes. Remove the baklava from the oven and immediately spoon the syrup over it. Let cool completely before serving. Store uncovered.

Greek Reading & Listening

The Mystery of History Volume I: Creation to the Resurrection by Linda Lacour Hobar (Bright Ideas Press) Chapters 1-3

Ancient Civilizations & The Bible by Diana Waring (Answers in Genesis) Unit 1

Streams of Civilization Volume I by Mary Stanton & Albert Hyma (Christian Liberty Press) Introductions & Chapter 1

History of the World in Christian Perspective by Jerry H. Combee (A'Beka Book) Chapter 1

Aesop's Fables by Aesop

Hour of the Olympics by Mary Pope Osborn (Random House Books for Young Readers)

The Odyssey for Boys and Girls by AJ Church (Yesterday's Book)

The Iliad for Boys and Girls by AJ Church (Yesterday's Books)

The Iliad by Homer

The Odyssey by Homer

Tanglewood Tales by Nathaniel Hawthorne

Famous Men of Greece by John Haaren and AB Poland (Greenleaf Press)

The Librarian Who Measured the Earth by Kathryn Lasky (Little Brown Books for Young Readers)

Usborne: The Greeks by Susan Peach & Anne Millard (Usborne)

Archimedes and the Door of Science by Jeanne Bendick (Bethlehem Books)

Audio CDs

What in the World is Going on Here? Volume 1: Ancient Civilizations and the Bible Disc 3 Track 5-7

Digger Deeper Volume 1: Ancient Civilizations and the Bible Disc 2 Track 4-5

Movies

Ulysses (1954)

Greek City-States Menu

Lunch

Greek Leg of Lamb

Aesop's Lemon Rice Pilaf

Golden Age Baklava

Lunch

Plato's Spanakopita (Greek Spinach Pie)

Pythagoras' Cinnamon Right Triangles

Marathon Honey Puffs

Lunch

Pythagoras' Garlic Right Triangles

Golden Age Gyro Pita Wrap

Pericles' Vasilopita

Roman Empire & Israel's Messiah

The Roman Republic

The king of Rome was overthrown in 509 B.C. and was replaced with a republican form of government.

Ancient Rome was a Republic from 509 B.C. to 45 B.C., ruled by elected senators who served for a limited amount of time. They had a constitution, a balance of power, and written laws. Though slaves had no rights, freemen could vote and have a say in their government.

The highest position in government was the consul. To limit his power, two consuls served at the same time.

During the Roman Republic centuries, Rome faced destruction when Hannibal invaded with his Carthage army by crossing the Alps on elephants. (The Second Punic War)

The Roman Empire

The Republic came to an abrupt end when Julius Caesar took over the Senate and made himself dictator for life, but was assassinated a year later. In 27 B.C. Caesar Augustus became the first Roman Empire. The Roman Republic was over and the mighty empire began to extend its kingdom.

Roman Engineering & Building

The Romans were amazing engineers and builders. They built thousands of miles of road, including 29 highways that connected important cities to Rome. That's why we still have the saying, "All roads lead to Rome." The roads were built with a hump causing water to flow to the edges.

Via is the Latin word for road. So roads were named something like this: Via Corinth, or Corinth Road.

Hundreds of bridges were built in the Roman Empire, many of which are still standing today. Bridges were built of stone and concrete. Arches made the bridges strong.

The Romans used domes and arches to create high ceilings with wide open spaces.

Middle class and wealthy people lived in villas, or fancy houses with many rooms and courtyards. The greatest building project of the Romans was the Coliseum, a huge outdoor stadium that seated 50,000 people who came to watch gladiator games, mock battles, and plays.

Aqueducts were long channels built to carry water into cities for drinking water, baths, and sewers. Roman plumbing was very advanced.

Roman Numerals

We still use Roman numerals today, especially when writing outlines. Here is a list of numbers 1-10, Roman numeral style:

I, II, III, IV, V, VI, VI, VII, VIII, IX, X.

Here are some of the other important numbers:

I = 1

V = 5

X = 10

L = 50

C = 100

D = 500

M = 1,000

Latin

The Latin language was the official language of the Roman Republic and Roman Empire. Latin remained an important intellectual language for centuries and many great works were written in Latin. Latin also developed into the Romance languages such as Spanish, France, Portuguese, and Italian.

Many words in English have Latin roots.

Roman Food

The Romans ate three meals a day. Lentaculum (breakfast) was a light meal of bread and fruit. Prandium (lunch) was another light meal eaten late morning. Cena (dinner) was the big meal and it was eaten in the late afternoon.

Romans enjoyed a wide variety of beef, pork, lamb, chicken, fish, oysters, bread, cheese, eggs, lentils, cucumbers, onions, lettuce, garlic, apples, figs, nuts, dates, honey, and cakes. They also ate flamingo tongues, dormice, roasted peacock, and stewed snails. They drank wine, often watered down.

At formal dinner banquets, they lay on their sides to eat. For casual meals, the Romans would sit on a stool or stand. They loved sauces with their food.

Jesus Christ, the Messiah, the Anointed One

"In the beginning was the Word, and the Word was with God, and the Word was God. He was in the beginning with God. All things came into being through Him, and apart from Him nothing came into being that has come into being. In Him was life, and the life was the Light of men. The Light shines in the darkness, and the darkness did not comprehend it" (John 1:1-5 NASB).

From the beginning, before the earth was created, Jesus was God and was with God. Right after Rome became an empire, a miracle happened in one of the Roman provinces, in Bethlehem, near Jerusalem. It was the greatest event in history.

Jesus' Birth

Jesus Christ was born in Bethlehem over 2,000 years ago to a virgin named Mary. His real father was God Himself. What?! Yes, it's true. Jesus Christ is fully human and fully God. It is so hard to wrap your mind around it, isn't it? You see, Jesus is the Messiah that was promised to the Jewish people. He is God in the flesh, the hope of all mankind.

Jesus' birth was announced by an angel named Gabriel to a young virgin named Mary, who was engaged to a righteous man named Joseph. Mary was a little dazed, but grateful for God's choosing her to be the mother of the long-awaited Messiah. When Joseph found out Mary was pregnant, he wanted to divorce her quietly, but God appeared to him in a dream so he took Mary as his wife. They traveled together to pay taxes in Bethlehem where Jesus was born in a stable because the city hotels were all full since everyone from the line of David was returning to Bethlehem to pay taxes.

Jesus' Life

Jesus grew up as an obedient son to his parents, who were the perfect parents for the Son of God. He learned the trade of carpentry from His father. Jesus was able to provide for His brothers and sisters financially as a carpenter after Joseph died until His ministry began.

Jesus was led by His Father to be baptized by His cousin, John the Baptist. As He was coming out of the water, the Holy Spirit descended on Him in the form of a dove. God the Father spoke words of affirmation over His Son Jesus, "This is my beloved Son. In Him I am well-pleased."

Immediately following His baptism, the Holy Spirit led Jesus out to the desert to fast for forty days and forty nights. After these forty days, Satan tempted Him. But Jesus refuted each temptation with Scripture.

One of Jesus' first miracles was at a wedding in Cana where He turned water into wine when the host ran out of wine before the party was over. But, most of Jesus' early ministry was preaching and teaching in the synagogues across Israel. Wherever He went, Jesus taught people about the Lord and how to live a righteous life. He spoke with love and authority.

Jesus also told many stories to help people understand what He was teaching. He made complex truths simple. He told jokes in the midst of His sermons and was a favorite of the children.

Miracles happened wherever Jesus went. People came to him with deformities, blindness, deafness, leprosy, and seizures. Jesus healed them all. What excitement surrounded His every move! Some of the people who had been healed followed Him as He traveled around Israel preaching the Good News of the Kingdom of God.

Demonized men and women were delivered from their bondage when Jesus and His disciples cast out demons. Yes, Jesus had disciples, or students, who traveled with Him. They learned from Him, watched Him, and were sent out by Him on trial runs to preach repentance and the Kingdom of God.

Jesus had many close friends, including Mary, Martha, and Lazarus. Near the end of His life, Jesus' friend Lazarus died from a sickness. When Jesus finally arrived at his house, He raised Lazarus from the dead! Wow! How exciting it was for His friends!

Many more miracles took place. Jesus walked on water. He fed huge crowds of people. He stilled storms. Most of all, Jesus healed broken hearts and broken lives. Wherever He went, there was transformation. Jesus turned the nation of Israel upside-down. However, things took a turn after three years of ministry.

Jesus' Death & Resurrection

Jesus celebrated the Passover with His disciples. He washed their feet and told them to celebrate Communion in the future to remember His death and resurrection.

After dinner and a time of worship, Jesus and His disciples went to the Garden of Gethsemane. He prayed for every one of His believers, present and future. He prayed for you and me! Then, He cried out to God in agony about His upcoming Heavenly Assignment. You see, Jesus had come to earth on a Mission. His mission was a rescue operation. He would take the weight of the world's sin on Himself and die on the cross to redeem mankind.

The events that followed were full of terror and torture. Jesus was arrested, endured a trial that was a mockery, and was sentenced to death. He had to carry his own cross to the place of crucifixion after being beaten with whips.

On the cross, He forgave His murderers, asked John to take care of His mother, and declared, "It is finished!" He paid the price of the world's sin. He was the Perfect Sacrifice, the Lamb that was slain. His followers took the body, prepared it for burial, and buried Jesus in a large tomb. Roman guards were stationed at the tomb to stop anything weird from happening. But, God was not finished yet!

Early Sunday morning, the stone was rolled away, and Jesus came out of the tomb! Jesus had risen from the dead! Jesus conquered death and sin for you and me! After His resurrection, Jesus spent several weeks with His disciples, getting them ready for His final departure. He ascended right up into the sky to Heaven and was gone! But, very soon, God poured out His Holy Spirit on the 120 believers who were praying and fasting in the Upper Room in Jerusalem. Then the work of His Glorious Church began and continues to this day. Jesus was with His disciples through the Holy Spirit. His work continued on by the power of the Holy Spirit.

Jesus, our King

Jesus is our King. The Bible calls Him the King of Kings. Jesus does all things well including running the universe and running our lives. Jesus is worshipped by angels, nature, and people He has rescued sinners and turned them into saints. His Kingdom is eternal. It will last forever. A million years from now we will still be worshipping our King Jesus!

Jesus, the Law Giver and Fulfiller

Jesus Fulfilled the Law. He is our Righteousness. What does that mean? Jesus obeyed every single command in Scripture perfectly. He never slacked off. He never compromised. In this way, He was able to be the Perfect Sacrifice. By meeting the righteous requirements of the law, Jesus fulfilled the Law.

When Jesus taught about the Law, he took it to a higher plane. He revealed true virtue, rather than just legalistic adherence to a bunch of rules. Jesus taught us that God is looking at our hearts. When Jesus changes our hearts, we will want to do what is right, fulfilling the Old Testament promise that God would write His Word on our hearts.

Jesus, our Judge

One day every knee will bow and every tongue confess that Jesus is Lord to the glory of God the Father we are told in Philippians chapter two in *The Holy Bible*. Everyone will acknowledge that Jesus is Lord, that no one is higher.

Jesus will also judge the living and the dead. Every person will stand before Jesus as his, or her, judge.

Jesus Loves You!

You, dear friend, were the joy set before Jesus when He endured the cross. He died so that your sins could be forgiven and wiped away if you repent and believe. Jesus had an unique heavenly assignment for you. He stands at the door and knocks. Don't miss out knowing the One who loves you best! Jesus is the Alpha and Omega, the Bright Morning Star, the Everlasting Father, Mighty God, our Good Shepherd, and the Risen Lamb. Get to know Him and you will experience the true joy in life!

"Behold, I stand at the door and knock; if anyone hears My voice and opens the door, I will come in to him and will dine with him and he with Me," Revelation 3:20 NASB).

Jesus' Twelve Apostles

Jesus chose twelve men that he worked with very closely, preparing them to take His Good News to the ends of the earth: Andrew, Nathanael, John, James brother of John, James, Judas, Thaddeus, Matthew, Simon Peter, Philip, Simon the Zealot, and Thomas. Except for Judas who betrayed Jesus and committed suicide, the disciples received the Great Commission in Galilee and watched Jesus ascend into Heaven. They waited in Jerusalem for the promised Holy Spirit and spent their lives sharing the Gospel.

Jesus' brother James became a leader in the church. Paul, a former persecutor of Christians, was radically converted and traveled the rest of his life to preach the Good News. The Gospel spread around Asia, into Africa, and all the way to Europe. Local churches were established everywhere that people got saved.

According to tradition, this is how the other eleven apostle died. James was the first apostle martyred. The other James was sawn in pieces. Andrew was crucified and Peter was crucified upside-down. Thaddeus was killed with arrows. Simon was martyred. Thomas was killed with a spear. Nathanael was flayed alive with knives. Philip was hung. Matthew was martyred in Ethiopia. John was the only one who died of natural causes.

The Early Church

The early church was devoted to the Lord, His teachings, prayer, and each other. Being a Christian could mean death and many Christians lost their lives because of their faith. But, in spite of persecution, the Good News traveled and people who wanted to be free from their sins and experience forgiveness from God repented, believed, and were transformed.

Churches sprang up in cities throughout the Roman Empire. Leaders were raised up. Needs were met. New believers were baptized.

With the Greeks spreading their language throughout parts of Asia, Europe, and Africa, there was now a common language to share the Good News everywhere. How to get there? Why not take the roads the Romans built. And so, in the perfect time, God sent Jesus and we have the privilege of taking the Good News to all the nations, just like the original disciples got to do.

John & Polycarp

For over thirty years, Apostle John ministered in Ephesus. Afterward, he was exiled to Patmos. He discipled Polycarp, who accepted Christ as a young child, and ordained him as Bishop of Smyrna. For 86 years, Polycarp served the Lord until he was arrested and threatened with death unless he renounced Christ. He refused to dishonor Christ and was burned to death. Polycarp was a teacher of Truth and helped to lay the foundation of the early Church.

Apostolic Fathers

Along with Polycarp, Clement of Rome and Ignatius of Antioch are considered Apostolic Fathers of the Church. Bishop of Rome, Clement is considered the first Pope by the Roman Catholic Church. He was consecrated as the fourth Bishop of Rome. Ignatius accepted Christ as a young boy and, along with Polycarp, was a disciple of John. Tradition says that he was one of the children that Jesus blessed. Ignatius was martyred by wild beasts. All three of the Apostolic Fathers wrote many letters to the churches, in the tradition of Paul, John, and Peter.

Eusebius

Eusebius, Bishop of Caesarea (260-340) and Father of Church History, wrote a chronological account of church history from the first century to the fourth century. He shares information about church leaders, battling heresies, Jewish history, martyrdoms, and treatment of the Church by the world. His book is divided up by according to the reigns of different emperors, except for the first section on Jesus Christ.

Coconut Bread

3 Cups Flour, sifted

1 Cup Shredded Coconut

1 Tbsp. Baking Powder

1 Egg, beaten

½ tsp. Salt

1 Cup Milk

1 Cup Sugar

1 tsp. Vanilla

Sift dry ingredients and add coconut. Mix thoroughly. Combine liquid ingredients, blend carefully. Let stand for 20 minutes. (Do NOT skip this step!) Pour into well greased pan (9"x5"x3") and bake at 350° for 45-50 minutes (For more chewy texture, bake 60 minutes!) This is BETTER not sliced until the NEXT day!

Italian Herb Bread

1¼ Cups Water

4⅓ Cups Bread Flour

1 tsp. Salt

2 Tbsp. Sugar

2 Tbsp. Dry Milk

2 Tbsp. Butter

1 ½ tsp. Dried Marjoram

1 ½ tsp. Dried Basil

1 ½ tsp. Dried Thyme

1 ½ tsp. Yeast

Place ingredients in bread maker in the order listed. Set bread maker on the French Bread setting for a 2# loaf. Serve with butter.

John the Baptist Whole Wheat Honey Bread

1½ Cups Water

3¼ Cups Whole Wheat Flour

1 Cup Corn Meal

2 tsp. Salt

½ Cup Honey

1 ½ Tbsp. Dry Milk

2 Tbsp. Butter

1 ¾ tsp Yeast

Place ingredients in bread maker in the order listed. Set breadmaker on the whole wheat setting for a 2# loaf.

Roman Boiled Eggs

12 Eggs, boiled and chopped

¼ Cup Pine Nuts

9 Tbsp. Vinegar

3 Tbsp. Honey

Salt, Pepper, & Garlic Powder to taste

Soak pine nuts in vinegar for 3-4 hours. Mix pine nuts, vinegar, honey, salt, pepper, and garlic powder in a food processor. Mix with chopped eggs.

Cleopatra's Fish Chowder

2 Pounds Frozen Fish Filets (catfish, haddock, etc.)

1/4 lb. Bacon, diced

1 Medium Onion, chopped

4 Medium Potatoes, peeled and cubed

2 Cups Water

Salt, to taste

Pepper, to Taste

1 Can (12 ounces) Evaporated Milk

Thaw frozen fish in refrigerator. Cut into bite-sized pieces. In skillet, saute bacon and onion until meat is cooked and onion is golden. Drain and put into Crock Pot with the fish pieces. Add potatoes, water, salt, and pepper. Cover and cook on low for 5 to 8 hours. Add evaporated milk during last hour.

Julius Caesar Drumsticks

8 Drumsticks

1 Cup Flour

2 tsp. Ground Cumin

2 tsp. Caraway Seeds

2 tsp. Sweet Paprika Powder

1 Tbsp. Honey

2 Bay Leaves

Vegetable Oil

Fill a gallon-size zippered plastic bag with flour, cumin, bay leaves, caraway seeds, and paprika. Cover each drumstick with a light coat of oil. Toss drumsticks into bag and shake until they are covered with flour mixture. Open bag and drizzle in honey. Close bag and toss again. Store in refrigerator overnight so flavors can soak in. The next day, bake drumsticks on greased baking pan at 350°F until chicken cooked through.

Sea of Galilee Tilapia

3 Lemons

2 Pounds Tilapia or Flounder Fillets

Salt and Pepper

Fresh Mint Leaves, thinly sliced

1 Golden Delicious Apple, cored and cut into 1/2-inch-long matchstick strips

¼ Cup(s) Green Olives, pitted and thinly sliced

1 Green Onion, thinly sliced

½ tsp. Sugar

½ tsp. Lemon Peel

Preheat oven to 450 degrees F. Arrange tilapia fillets in 13" by 9" glass baking dish. Sprinkle with lemon juice, salt, and pepper. Roast Tilapia 8 to 10 minutes, or until just opaque throughout.

Meanwhile, prepare relish from remaining lemon, lemon peel, mint leaves, apple, olives, shallot, and sugar. Serve relish with tilapia; sprinkle with mint.

Tomatoes Stuffed with Roman Rice

8 Large Tomatoes, rinsed and patted dry

4 Cups Cooked Rice

1 Clove Garlic, minced

1 tsp. Basil

1 tsp. Parsley

Olive Oil

Salt and Pepper to taste

Cut around the tops of the tomatoes and carefully scoop out the pulp and the juice of tomatoes. Place the hallowed tomatoes in a baking dish. Mix rice, basil, parsley, salt, pepper, and olive oil together. Fill tomato cups with rice mixture. Bake at 350° for 30 minutes.

Hannibal's Sweet and Nutty Couscous

2 Cups Chicken Broth

1 Stick Butter

1/3 Cup Chopped Dates

1/3 Cup Chopped Dried Apricots

1/3 Cup Golden Raisins

2 Cups Dry Couscous

3 tsp. Ground Cinnamon

½ Cup Slivered Almonds, toasted

Pour the broth into a large saucepan, and bring to a boil. Add the butter, apricots, dates and raisins. Boil for 2 to 3 minutes. Remove from the heat, and stir in the couscous. Cover, and let stand for 5 minutes. Stir in the cinnamon and toasted almonds, and serve.

Alexander the Great's Rice Pilaf

Rice pilaf was first discovered in some letters written by Alexander the Great about his visits with the Persians.

½ Cup Butter

8 Cups Chicken Broth

1 Cup Chopped Onions

4 Cups Uncooked Brown or White Rice

Melt the butter in a pan over medium heat. Cook onion in butter until clear. Stir in rice and cook for 5 minutes, stirring frequently. Stir in broth. Heat to boiling; reduce to low. Cover and simmer for 15 minutes. Remove from heat and let it stand for 5 minutes.

Maccabean Apricot-Raspberry Rugelach

1 Cup Butter, softened

1 Package (8 ounces) Cream Cheese, softened

1 tsp. Vanilla

¼ tsp. Salt

2 Cups Flour

¾ Cups Sugar

1 Cup Walnuts, chopped

¾ Cup Chopped Apricots, chopped

¼ Cup Packed Light Brown Sugar

1 ½ tsp. Ground Cinnamon

2 Cups Seedless Raspberry Preserves

1 Tbsp. Milk

In large bowl, beat butter with cream cheese until blended and smooth. Beat in vanilla, salt, 1 cup flour, and 1/4 cup sugar until blended. With spoon, stir in remaining flour. Divide dough into 4 equal pieces. Wrap each with plastic wrap and refrigerate until firm, at least 2 hours or overnight.

Prepare filling: In medium bowl, with spoon, stir walnuts, apricots, brown sugar, 1/4 cup plus 2 tablespoons sugar, and 1/2 teaspoon cinnamon until well mixed. Line 2 large cookie sheets with foil; grease foil.

On lightly floured surface, with floured rolling pin, roll 1 piece of chilled dough into a 9-inch round, keeping remaining dough refrigerated. Spread dough with 2 tablespoons raspberry preserves. Sprinkle with about 1/2 cup apricot filling; gently press filling onto dough. With pastry wheel or sharp knife, cut dough into 12 equal wedges. Starting at curved edge, roll up each wedge, jelly-roll fashion. Place cookies on foil-lined cookie sheet, point-side down, about 1/2 inch apart. Repeat with remaining dough, one-fourth at a time.

Preheat oven to 325 degrees F. In cup, mix remaining 2 tablespoons sugar with 1 teaspoon cinnamon. With pastry brush, brush rugelach with milk. Sprinkle with cinnamon-sugar.

Bake rugelach on 2 oven racks about 30 to 35 minutes until golden, rotating cookie sheets between upper and lower racks halfway through baking time. Immediately remove rugelach to wire racks to cool. Store in tightly covered container.

Caesar Augustus Baked Cheesecake

Crust:

1 ¼ Cup Graham-Cracker Crumbs

2 Tbsp. Sugar

¼ Cup Butter, melted

Cheese Mixture:

4 (8-oz.) Pkgs. Cream Cheese

1 Cup Sugar

2 Eggs

¼ Cup All-Purpose Flour

1 tsp. Grated Lemon Peel

1 Cup Dairy Sour Cream

Topping:

1 tsp. Grated Lemon Peel

1 Can Cherry or Blueberry Pie Filling

1 Cup Dairy Sour Cream

Preheat oven to 350°F. Grease a 9-in. spring form pan. In a small bowl combine cracker crumbs and sugar. Stir in butter. Press crumbs onto bottom of pan. Bake 10 min. Remove. Cool on wire rack. Increase oven to 400°F. In large bowl beat cream cheese & sugar until smooth. Beat in eggs, flour & lemon peel until blended. Stir in sour cream. Pour cheese mixture over bottom crust. Smooth top. Bake 45-50 minutes or until center is set. Turn oven off; leave cheesecake in cooling oven with door slightly ajar, 3 hours. Remove from oven. Cool completely in pan on a wire rack. Refrigerate until served. To serve, run tip of knife around inside edge of pan. Release and remove pan side. Place cheesecake on a serving plate. Pour pie filling over top of cake, spreading to cover the whole top.

Roman Empire & Israel's Messiah Reading & Listening

The Mystery of History Volume I: Creation to the Resurrection by Linda Lacour Hobar (Bright Ideas Press) Chapters 1-3

Ancient Civilizations & The Bible by Diana Waring (Answers in Genesis) Unit 1

Streams of Civilization Volume I by Mary Stanton & Albert Hyma (Christian Liberty Press) Introductions & Chapter 1

History of the World in Christian Perspective by Jerry H. Combee (A'Beka Book) Chapter 1

Royal Diaries: Cleopatra VII, Daughter of the Nile by Kristianna Gregory (Scholastic)

About The History of the Calendar by A. E. Evenson (Children's Press)

The Runaway by Patricia St John (Christian Focus Publications)

Twice Freed by Patricia St John (Christian Focus Publications)

Fountain of Life by Rebecca Martin (Christian Light Publications)

The Bronze Bow by Elizabeth George Speare (Sandpiper)

Ben Hur by Lew Wallace (Signet Classics)

Titus: A Comrade of the Cross by Florence Morse Kingsley (Lamplighter Publishing)

Augustus Caesar's World by Genevieve Foster (Beautiful Feet Books)

Famous Men of Rome by John Haaren & AB Poland (Greenleaf Press)

Usborne Time Traveller: Rome & Romans by Heather Amery and Patricia Vanags (E. D. C. Publishing)

"I and II Macabees" from *The Apocrypha*

"Julius Caesar" by William Shakespeare

Life Stories from Plutarch's Lives

Pompeii….Buried Alive! by Edith Kunhardt (Random House Books for Young Readers)

The Robe by Lloyd C Douglas (Mariner Books)

Audio CDs

What in the World is Going on Here? Volume 1: Ancient Civilizations and the Bible Disc 3 Track 8, Disc 4 Track 1-8

True Tales Volume 1: Ancient Civilizations and the Bible Disc 3 Track 3

Digger Deeper Volume 1: Ancient Civilizations and the Bible Disc 2 Track 6-9, Disc 3 Track 1-7

Movies

Julius Caesar (1953—Marlon Brando)

Cleopatra (starring Elizabeth Taylor)

Spartacus (Kirk Douglas)

Ben Hur

Passion (A Mel Gibson Film)

Jesus (Campus Crusade)

The Gospel of John (Visual Bible)

The Robe (1953 Starring Richard Burton)

Roman Empire & Israel's Messiah Menu

Lunch

Julius Caesar Drumsticks

Alexander the Great Rice Pilaf

Coconut Bread

Lunch

Roman Boiled Eggs

Hannibal's Sweet & Nutty Couscous

Maccabean Apricot-Raspberry Rugelach

Lunch

Cleopatra's Fish Chowder

John the Baptist Whole Wheat Bread

Caesar Augustus Cheesecake

Lunch

Sea of Galilee Tilapia

Tomato Cups with Roman Rice

Resurrection Cookies

Resources

Our Co-op Lesson Plans

Powerline Productions

World History I Co-op Lesson Plans

Creation, Flood & Early Civilizations

Week One Creation

Homework: *The Mystery of History Volume I: Creation to the Resurrection* by Linda Lacour Hobar Read aloud pg 6-13

Listen to **What in the World is Going on Here** Volume I Tape 1 Creation to the Destruction of Assyria (A)   {Discuss tape pg. 61)

Lunch: Garden of Eden Salad, Seth's Favorite Fruit Salad, Eve's Apple and Walnut Salad, Fruit Smoothies

Worship, Memory Work, and Reports: *All Things Bright and Beautiful, All Creatures of our God and King, How Great Thou Art* & September Book oral reports

Look at World History Timeline….play game!

Read Aloud *Dinosaurs in God's World and Long Ago*

Read Aloud *What Happened to the Dinosaurs?*

World Map

Watch Unlocking the Mystery of Life (60 min) or Icons of Evolution (80 min)

Ancient Civilizations and the Bible

 pg. 44 Art Appreciation: "The Sistine Chapel---**The Creation of Adam**" by Michaelangelo Buonarroti and Thomas Cole, *The Expulsion From the Garden of Eden!*
 pg. 49 Compose a song or poem called "You and me and the Forbidden Tree"

 Complete limerick about Cain

 pg. 51 Pantomime six days of creation

 pg. 51 Create a game that will help children remember the days of creation events.

Ancient Civilizations Elementary Activity Book pg. 8 Sing "On Day One"

Sing *All Things Bright and Beautiful, How Great Thou Art, All Creatures of our God and King*

Wk Two Flood, Ice Age, Dinosaurs

Homework: *The Mystery of History Volume I: Creation to the Resurrection* by Linda Lacour Hobar. Read aloud pg17-25

Listen *An In Depth Study of Noah's Ark*

Lunch: Dinosaur Nuggets, Pterodactyl Wings, Ice Age Slushies,

Worship, Memory Work, and Reports: *Arky, Arky, All Creatures of our God and King,*

Read Aloud *In the Days of Noah*

Read Aloud *Life in the Great Ice Age*

ART APPRECIATION: Jan Brueghel, the elder, ***Entry of the Animals into Noah's Ark!*** And Diane Renis Design's ***Leopards and the Ark!*** Edward Hicks, ***Noah's Ark*** (*Ancient Civilizations and the Bibile* pg. 44).

Ancient Civilizations and the Bible

> pg. 42 Map exercise
>
> pg. 44 Art Appreciation: "Noah's Ark" by Edward Hicks
>
> pg. 46 Do it yourself flood in a jar
>
> pg. 50 Use puppets to tell story of Noah's Ark and flood

Wk Three Tower of Babel, Sumerians, Stonehenge, Epic of Gilgamesh, Early Egyptians, Minoans

Homework: *The Mystery of History Volume I: Creation to the Resurrection* by Linda Lacour Hobar Read aloud pages 27-44.

Listen to ***True Tales: Ancient Civilizations and the Bible*** (A. Table of Nations; Discovery of Troy; Discovery of Ur) {Discuss pg.61)

Lunch: Peanut Butter Playdough Tablets, Minoan Fruit Cup, Stonehenge Dessert (Hannah Cake)

Worship, Memory Work, and Reports: *Awesome God, How Great Thou Art*

Mesopotamia Map

The Mystery of History Volume I: Creation to the Resurrection by Linda Lacour Hobar.

Pg. 42 Bull Leaping

Pg. 30 Experience the Tower of Babel

Pg. 28 Make a cuneiform tablet

Ancient Civilizations and the Bible

pg. Write a song about Nimrod to tune of *Camptown Races*.

Wk Four Patriarchs, Hammurabi, China & Shang Dynasty, Slaves in Egypt

Homework: *The Mystery of History Volume I: Creation to the Resurrection* by Linda Lacour Hobar Read aloud pg 46-62

Lunch: Esau's Lentil Stew, Jacob's Ladder Angel Biscuits, Abraham's Descendant Star Cookies,

Sing *"Father Abraham"*

Read aloud *Magic School Bus: Shows and Tells* by Jackie Posner

Watch Video*: A Walk Through History* video from Institute of Creation Research (80 min.)

ART APPRECIATION: Rembrandt, *Jacob Blessing the Sons of Joseph*, *Pieter Bruegel*, *Tower of Babel*, *a*nd Diane Renis Degign's *Jacobs Ladder!*

Ancient Civilizations and the Bible

pg. 74 Map exercise

pg. 74 Art Appreciation: "Tower of Babel" by Pieter Bruegel

pg. 75 Imitate Bruegel

pg. 75 Construct a small city out of legos.

Crossroads in Time (Archaeology Activity Book) pg. 1-7 Do activity pages

Ancient Civilizations Elementary Activity Book pg. 19 We "Dig" Archaeology

Egypt & Nation of Israel

Week Five Exodus, Ark of Covenant, Joshua

Homework: *The Mystery of History Volume I: Creation to the Resurrection* by Linda Lacour Hobar Read aloud pages 64-73.

Listen to **What in the World is Going on Here?** Vol 1 Tape 1B finish!

Lunch: Promised Land Granola, Yogurt, Yogurt Cake with Frosting, Aaron's Rod Candy, Grapes, Hot Milk with Honey OR Passover Meal

The Mystery of History Volume I: Creation to the Resurrection by Linda Lacour Hobar Pg. 66 Ten Plagues Chart

   Pg. 71 Jericho March

Ancient Civilizations and the Bible

      pg. 99-100 Discuss Rosetta Stone, etc.

      pg. 111 Journalism: "Family Finds Long Lost Son"

      pg. 112 Real Estate Ad

      pg. 113 Act out Exodus

      pg. 138 Make Yogurt cake with frosting

Sing "Horse and Rider" and dance with tambourines

Look at Timeline of Israel

Read aloud *Miriam's Cup: A Passover Story* by Fran Manushkin

Learning about Passover by Barbara Soloff Levy

Watch Video: **The Ten Commandments** or The Prince of Egypt (1 hr. 39 minutes)

Ancient Civilizations Elementary Activity Book

      Pg. 28 Sing "Plagues are Plaguing

Week Six King Tut, Ramses II, Amenhotep, Nefertiti, Troy, Trojan Horse, Ruth, Gideon

Homework: *The Mystery of History Volume I: Creation to the Resurrection* by Linda Lacour Hobar Read aloud pg 75-93.

Listen to *More True Tales from Ancient Civilizations and the Bible* B (Mt. Sinai) and *True Tales from Ancient Civilizations and the Bible* A (Rosetta Stone)

Lunch: Ruth's Barley Squares, Nile Fish Sandwiches, Leek & Onion Soup,

The Mystery of History Volume I: Creation to the Resurrection by Linda Lacour Hobar. Complete worksheet pg. 93

Read aloud *Adventures in Ancient Egypt* by Linda Bailey

Look at *Six Egyptian Cards* from the Brooklyn Museum

Ancient Civilizations and the Bible

> pg. 141 Skit about Gideon
>
> **pg. 104 Map Exercise**
>
> Pg. 108-109 Music: Rhythm

1175 BC to 627 BC

Week Seven Samson, Zhou Dynasty, Samuel, Saul, David, Solomon

Homework: *The Mystery of History Volume I: Creation to the Resurrection* by Linda Lacour Hobar Read aloud pg 100-119

Lunch: David's Shepherd's Pie, Abigail's Raisin Cakes, Solomon's Honey Sesame Candy

Ancient Civilizations and the Bible

> Pg. 132 Map Exercise
>
> pg. 139 Limerick about Hiram
>
> pg. 140 Compose song about Queen Sheeba to "Comin Round the Mountain

pg. 142 Pantamime King David and the ark

Ancient Civilizations Elementary Activity Book

pg. 35 Krazy King's Game

Read aloud *Magnifications: The Temple at Jerusalem: From Solomon to Herod and Beyond*

Watch Video: *Samson and Delilah* (1949—starring Hedy Lamarr)

Week Eight Phoenicians, Israel Divides, Elijah, Joel, Obadiah, Homer

Homework: *The Mystery of History Volume I: Creation to the Resurrection* by Linda Lacour Hobar Read aloud pg 121-138.

Lunch: Elijah's Hummus with pita bread or crackers, cucumber salad or sliced cucumbers, Scripture Cake

The Mystery of History Volume I: Creation to the Resurrection by Linda Lacour Hobar

Copy Phoencian Alphabet Pg. 123

Ancient Civilizations and the Bible

Read Aloud *The Usborne Story of Painting* by Anthea Peppin

Make something out of purple cloth

Crossroads in Time (Archaeology Activity Book) pages. 9-17 Do activity pages

Assyrians, Babylonians, Persians, & More

Week Nine India & Hinduism, Olympic Games, Jonah, Amos, City of Rome, Isaiah, Micah, Israel falls to Assyria

Homework: *The Mystery of History Volume I: Creation to the Resurrection* by Linda Lacour Hobar Read aloud pages 131-147.

Listen to **True Tales of Ancient Civilizations** C (Discovery of Ninevah)

Lunch: Ezekiel Bread, Beef Barley Soup, Fig Newtons

The Mystery of History Volume I: Creation to the Resurrection by Linda Lacour Hobar

> page 143 Hold our own Olympic Games

> Pg. 145 Eat fig newtons (Amos)

Ancient Civilizations and the Bible

> pg. 155-156 Discuss tape

> pg. 168 Map Exercise

> pg. 160-163 RESEARCH and WRITE REPORT:

>> Jim and Josh: Assyria and Babylon today

>> JA: Samaria

>> Zack: HX of Babylonia and Assyria to present

>> JR: Judah's captivity

>> Sarah:

>> Cody: Assyrian siege warfare

> Pg.175-176 Make Ezekiel Bread and Barley Soup

> Pg. 177 Finish Jonah Limerick

Watch Video: **Veggie Tales: JONAH** (83 minutes)

Week Ten Hosea, Hezekiah, Sennacheribe, Native Americans, Manasseh, Athens & Sparta, Mesopotamia

Homework: *The Mystery of History Volume I: Creation to the Resurrection* by Linda Lacour Hobar Read aloud pages 160-176.

Listen to *What in the World is Going on Here?* Vol. 1 Tape 2A (Assyria and Babylon)

Lunch: Hezekiah Celebrates the Passover with a Seder Plate, Charoset, Matzo Ball Chicken Soup, Almond Macaroons,

Listen to oral reports from JA, JR, SJ, Cody, P, J, J, and S.
Ancient Civilizations and the Bible

> pg. 155 Talk Together

> pg. 173-174 Music Timbre Activities

>> Listen to Peter and the Wolf

Read aloud *The Usborne Story of Music* by Simon Mundy

Ancient Civilizations Elementary Activity Book pg. 45 Act out Hezekiah and Sennacherib

Week Eleven King Josiah, Nahum, Zephaniah, Jeremiah

Homework: The Mystery of History Volume I: Creation to the Resurrection by Linda Lacour Hobar Read aloud page 179-188.

Listen to True Tales From Times of Ancient Civilizations C (Austen Layard and Discovery of Ninevah)

Lunch: Nahum's Challah Bread, King Josiah's Roasted Chicken, Zephaniah Pistachio Pudding Desert

Read Aloud *The Usborne Book of Living Long Ago: Everyday Life Through the Ages* by Felicity Brooks and Helen Edom

612 BC to 404 BC

Week Twelve Nineveh, Habakkuk, Babylon Captivity, Daniel, Nebuchadnezar and Hanging Gardens, Aesop's Fables

Homework: *The Mystery of History Volume I: Creation to the Resurrection* by Linda Lacour Hobar Read aloud pages 197-214.

Listen to *In Depth Study of the 7 Wonders of the Ancient World.*

Lunch: Shadrach's Veggie Crescent Roll Squares, Daniel's Veggie Bagel Pizza, Hanging Gardens Date Nut Bread

Ancient Civilizations and the Bible

> pg. 172 Draw Four Empires Picture from Daniel

> pg. 172 Painted Babylonian Walls

Ancient Civilizations Elementary Activity Book

> pg. 46 Sing "Old King Neb"

> pg. 177 Poetry with unit words

> Pg. 179 Puppet show about Daniel and the Vegetarians

Persians, Medes, & Greece

Week Thirteen Ezekiel, Buddha, Confucius, Pythagoras, Shadrach, Meshach, Abendigo, Cyrus

Homework: *The Mystery of History Volume I: Creation to the Resurrection* by Linda Lacour Hobar Read aloud pages 216-236.

Lunch: China Honey Glazed Chicken Wings, India EZ Fruity Macaroons, Pythagoras' Garlic or Cinnamon Right Triangles,

Ancient Civilizations Time Traveler: Greece Read and do activity sheets

Ancient Civilizations and the Bible

Pg. 243 Music pitch

Pg. 247 Compose, using Dorian mode.

Week Fourteen Darius, Zerubbabel, Haggai, Zachariah, Roman Republic, Battle of Marathon, Herodotus

Homework: *The Mystery of History Volume I: Creation to the Resurrection* by Linda Lacour Hobar Read aloud pages 239-256.

Listen to *What in the World is Going On Here Vol 1 Tape 2B* (Persians and Medes)

Lunch: Roman Republic Spaghetti and Meatballs or Greek Leg of Lamb, Darius Green Beans, Marathon Honey Puffs,

Ancient Civilizations and the Bible

Pg. 192-193 Discus

Pg. 202 Map Exercise

Pg. 206 Science Braided rope

Pg. 107 Music

Pg. 210 Design a T-shirt "We survived….."

Week Fifteen Xerxes I, Esther, Golden Age of Athens, Socrates, Hippocrates, Ezra, Artaxeres

Homework: *The Mystery of History Volume I: Creation to the Resurrection* by Linda Lacour Hobar. Read aloud pages 258-276.

Listen to *What in the World is Going On Here Vol 1 Tape 2C* (The Greeks and The Hellenistic Empire)

Lunch: Golden Age Gyros, Figs, Olives, Golden Age Baklava, Esther's Apple Cake

The Mystery of History Volume I: Creation to the Resurrection by Linda Lacour Hobar

Pg. 259 BOYS recreate floating bridge in bathtub

Pg. 261 GIRLS make-over

Pg. 263 Make a Greek Theater Mask with paper plates

Pg. 270 Dress Greek. Take pictures. Create picture with Greek columns and use us in them (clothing—white bedsheets)

Read aloud <u>Adventures in Ancient Greece</u> by Linda Bailey

Ancient Civilizations and the Bible

pg. 225-226 Talk together

pg. 238 Map Exercise

Finish limerick about Esther's uncle

Pg. 244 Make Baklava (and Gyros)

Ancient Civilizations Elementary Activity Book

pg. 57 & 60 Archimedes & Buoyancy

Watch video: Veggie Tales *Esther*

444 BC to AD 29

Week Sixteen Nehemiah, Pericles, Peloponnesian War, Malachi, Plato, Aristotle, Phillip II of Macedonia

Homework: *The Mystery of History Volume I: Creation to the Resurrection* by Linda Lacour Hobar Read aloud pages 277 & 291.

Lunch: Plato's Spanakopita (Greek Spinach Pie), Aristotle Greek Salad, Pericles' Vasilopita

Read aloud *The Librarian Who Measured the Earth* by Kathryn Lasky

ART APPRECIATION: Giorgione, *The Adoration of the Shepherds!*

Copy Greek root words and make poster (bios, para, chronos, astron, petros, geo, pyro, logos, phone, kinesis, philia, photos)

Ancient Civilizations and the Bible

pg. 240 Architecture

pg. 241 Draw Greek Columns

pg. 241 Greek Vase art

pg. 233 & 244 Aristotle and Scientific method

pg. 248 Comedy Skit: Award Banquet (JR, JA, Z, C, S) videotape

pg. 149 Pantomime of Alexander the Great wanting to ride Bucephalus (J, J, SJ, P) videotape

Perform skits for one another.

Ancient Civilizations Elementary Activity Book pg. 63 Pillow-Pony-Shawn War skit

Greece & Rome, JESUS CHRIST

Week Seventeen   Alexander the Great, Archimedes, India, Septuagint, Qin Dynasty of China

Homework: *The Mystery of History Volume I: Creation to the Resurrection* by Linda Lacour Hobar Read aloud pages 302-320.

Lunch: Chicken Curry, Alexander the Great Rice Pilaf, Coconut Bread

The Mystery of History Volume I: Creation to the Resurrection by Linda Lacour Hobar

Pg. 297 Make your own phalanx

Pg.   Count to ten in Hindi

Read Aloud *The Story about Ping* by Majorie Flack and Kurt Wiese

Read Aloud *Adventures in Ancient China* by Linda Bailey

Read Aloud *From Arasp to Zuni: A Book of Bibleless People* by Karen Lewis

Wycliffe Bible Translators Activities from Internet

Possible Field Trip to Wycliffe

Ancient Civilizations and the Bible

Watch video: *Julius Caesar (1953—Marlon Brando)*

Week Eighteen   Hannibal, Han Dynasty, Macabean Revolt, Spartacus, First Triumvirate, Julius Ceasar

Homework: *The Mystery of History Volume I: Creation to the Resurrection* by Linda Lacour Hobar. Read aloud pages 322-339.

Listen to *What in the World is Going on Here Volume 1 Tape 2D and E* (Rise of Rome and Jesus Christ!)

Lunch: Han Chinese Pepper Steak, Hannibal's Sweet and Nutty Couscous, Macabean Apricot-Raspberry Rugelach

The Mystery of History Volume I: Creation to the Resurrection by Linda Lacour Hobar

> Pg. 332 Slave sale with signs

> Copy Roman numerals, Copy Roman root words and make poster   (populus, frater, mater, pater, magnus, vivo, stella, annus, terra, tempus, vulcanus, agua),   Look at Roman Empire poster

Read aloud "I and II Macabees" from the *Apocrypha*

Ancient Civilizations and the Bible

> pg. 262 Talk Together

> pg. 274 Map Exercise

> pg. 276, 277, & 283 Design-a-City

Ancient Civilizations (Time Travelers): Rome read and do activity pages

Watch video: *Cleopatra* (starring Elizabeth Taylor) or *Spartacus* (Kirk Douglas)

Week Nineteen   Second Triumvirate, Herod, Battle of Actium, Cleopatra, Augustus Caesar, John the Baptist

Homework: *The Mystery of History Volume I: Creation to the Resurrection* by Linda Lacour Hobar Read aloud pages 341-363.

Listen to *More True Tales from Ancient Civilizations B* (Finish Tape   iblical Prophecies of Jesus Fulfilled)

Lunch: Cleopatra's Fish Chowder, Roman Boiled Eggs, John the Baptist Whole Wheat Bread, Caesar Augustus Cheesecake

The Mystery of History Volume I: Creation to the Resurrection by Linda Lacour Hobar

Exercise pg. 363

Ancient Civilizations and the Bible

pg. 293-294 Talk Together

pg. 302 Map Exercise

pg. 304 *"The Annunciation"* by Jan van Eyck

ART APPRECIATION: Hubert and Jan van Eyck, ***The Annunciation!***

Crossroads in Time (Archaeology Activity Book) pg. 19-32. Read and do activity pages

Watch Video: *BenHur* cartoon

Week Twenty Jesus, Jesus' Disciples & Death & Resurrection, Tiberius Caesar, Pilate, Herod

Homework: *The Mystery of History Volume I: Creation to the Resurrection* by Linda Lacour Hobar Read aloud pg 366-387

Lunch: Sea of Galilee Talapia, Tomato Cups with Roman Rice, Resurrection Cookies

The Mystery of History Volume I: Creation to the Resurrection by Linda Lacour Hobar

Complete Worksheet 4 pg. 387

Pg. 372 Arches Discuss architecture and engineering of an arch.

Pg. 383 Make Resurrection Cookies

Semester II Exam!!!

Read aloud *Bridges* by Henry Billings pg.34-36

ART APPRECIATION: Hubert and Jan van Eyck, *The Adoration of the Lamb!*

Watch DVD: *Passion* or *Jesus* or *The Robe*

Ancient Civilizations and the Bible

Pg. 307 Music: Listen to Handel's Messiah

Being World Changers!

Raising World Changers!

Powerline Productions exists to serve you! We want you to grow in your relationship with Jesus, experience joy and success in your homeschooling journey, and fulfill the Great Commission with your family in your home, church, and community.

We offer Homeschooling books, unit studies, classes, high school classes, ladies Bible study workbooks, God's Girls Bible study workbooks, Real Men Bible study workbooks, Worship CDs, teaching CDs, DVDs, and cookbooks just for you!

Our Websites

joyfulandsuccessfulhomeschooling.com/
jshomeschooling.com/
finishwellcon.com/
powerlineprod.com/
meredithcurtis.com/

E-books Available at powerlineprod.com/
currclick.com/browse/pub/247/Powerline-Productions

Print Books Available @ amazon.com/ **(look up Books by Title)**

Contact Us: Laura@powerlinecc.com **&** Meredith@powerlinecc.com &
PastorMike@powerlinecc.com

Powerline Productions
251 Brightview Drive Lake Mary, FL 32746

Teaching History the Fun Way

History shouldn't be dull and boring. HIS story is exciting! God is moving in the earth throughout time, preparing the way for his Son, and taking the Truth about Jesus to the end of the earth. You can see His Hand moving throughout the centuries. So, let's have fun with our kids as we introduce them the Grand Story, the battle between good and evil, the faithfulness of God. We have timelines, cookbooks, unit studies, lapbooks, and events for your family or homeschool co-op to enjoy.

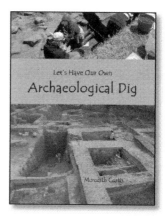

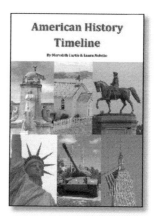

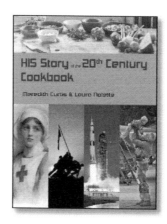
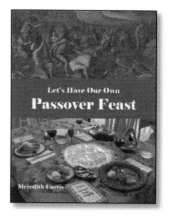

Ladies Bible Studies

The Word of God brings wisdom to woman in their roles as wives, mothers, homemakers, mentors, leaders, teachers, and businesswomen. Dig into Scripture and allow it to transform your life! Draw closer to Jesus and experience success as you walk in God's plan for your life!

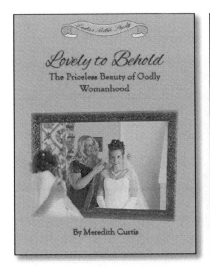
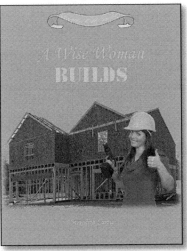
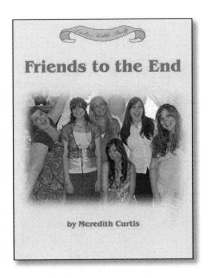

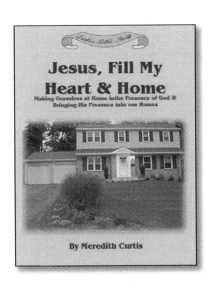

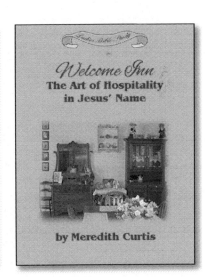

Maggie King Mysteries

If you like cozy mysteries, you will love this series! Meet Maggie King, a pastor's wife and homeschool mom who keeps stumbling across dead bodies. With her sidekicks, Sophia and Mary-Kate and her curious children, Maggie is on one adventure after another.

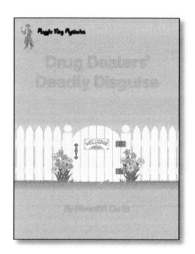

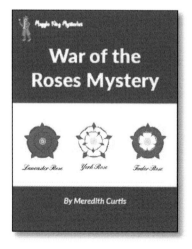
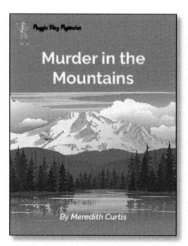

More Books by Powerline Productions

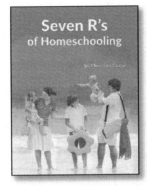  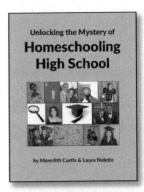 

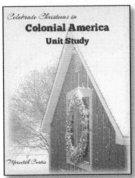   

More Books by Powerline Productions

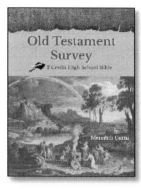

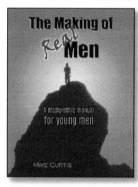

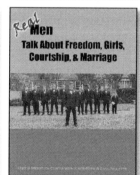

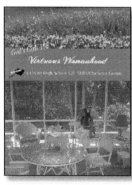

BOUT THE AUTHOR

Meredith Curtis, a pastor's wife and homeschooling mom of five amazing children, leads worship, mentors ladies, and, sometimes, even cooks dinner. Her passion is to equip people to love Jesus, raise godly children, and change the world around them with the power of the Gospel. "Lives are changed in the context of relationships," Meredith often says, as well as, "Be a world changer! Raise world changers!" She enjoys speaking to small and large groups.

All inquiries can be made to the author, Meredith Curtis, through email: Meredith@powerlinecc.com or contact her through her websites:
joyfulandsuccessfulhomeschooling.com/
meredithcurtis.com/
finishwellcon.com/
powerlineprod.com/
Meredith is the author of several books.
Joyful and Successful Homeschooling
Seven R's of Homeschooling
Quick & EZ Unit Study Fun
Unlocking the Mysteries of Homeschooling High School (with Laura Nolette)
Celebrate Thanksgiving
Teaching Writing in High School with Classes You Can Use
Teaching Literature in High School with Classes You Can Use
HIS Story of the 20th Century
HIS Story of the 20th Century for Little Folks

Meredith is the author of several cozy mysteries: The Maggie King Mysteries series.
Drug Dealers Deadly Disguise
Hurricanes Can Be Deadly
Legend of the Candy Cane Murder
Wash, Dry, Cut, & Die
War of the Roses Mystery
Murder in the Mountains

Meredith is the author of several Bible studies.
Lovely to Behold
A Wise Woman Builds
Jesus, Fill My Heart & Home
Welcome Inn: Practicing the Art of Hospitality in Jesus" Name
Friends to the End
God's Girls Beauty Secrets (with Sarah Jeffords)
God's Girls Friends to the End (with Katie-Beth Nolette & Sarah Jeffords)

God's Girls Talk about Boys, Dating, Courtship, & Marriage

Meredith is the author of several unit studies, timelines, and cookbooks.
Celebrate Christmas in Colonial America
Celebrate Christmas with Cookies
Travel to London Unit Study
Celebrate Thanksgiving with the Pilgrims Unit Study
American History Cookbook
Ancient History Cookbook
20th Century Cookbook (with Laura Nolette)
20th Century Timeline (with Laura Nolette)
American History Timeline (with Laura Nolette)
Ancient History Timeline (with Laura Nolette)

Meredith is the author of several high school classes.
American Literature and Research
British Literature and Writing
Who Dun It: Murder Mystery Literature & Writing
Communication 101: Essays and Speeches
Foundations of Western Literature
Economics, Finances, and Business
Worldview 101: Understand the Times
New Testament Survey
Old Testament Survey
Great Commission

And more…

Made in the USA
Las Vegas, NV
14 August 2021